SAINTLY MOMS

Saintly MOMS

25 STORIES OF HOLINESS

KELLY ANN GUEST

Our Sunday Visitor
Huntington, Indiana

Nihil Obstat
Msgr. Michael Heintz, Ph.D.
Censor Librorum

Imprimatur
✠ Kevin C. Rhoades
Bishop of Fort Wayne-South Bend
August 5, 2021

The *Nihil Obstat* and *Imprimatur* are official declarations that a book is free from doctrinal or moral error. It is not implied that those who have granted the *Nihil Obstat* and *Imprimatur* agree with the contents, opinions, or statements expressed.

Our Sunday Visitor Publishing Division, Our Sunday Visitor, Inc., 200 Noll Plaza, Huntington, IN 46750; www.osv.com; 1-800-348-2440

ISBN: 978-1-68192-414-4 (Inventory No. T2309)
RELIGION—Christianity—Saints & Sainthood.
RELIGION—Christian Life—Family.
RELIGION—Christianity—Catholic.
eISBN: 978-1-68192-415-1
LCCN: 2021937981

Cover design and Interior design: Amanda Falk
Cover art and Interior art: AdobeStock

PRINTED IN THE UNITED STATES OF AMERICA

*This book is dedicated to the many mothers
with whom God has blessed me:*

*First and foremost, my own saintly mom, Catherine
(Cookie) Hauf, who taught me through her
example how to love every person as a child of
God and how to suffer with joyful resignation.*

*For my mother-in-law, Diana Guest, who, though
not Catholic herself, always supports me in
everything, and always encourages her son, my
husband, to go to Mass with us. Thanks, Mom!*

*For my mother in religious life, Sister Mary Angela
Highfield, OP, who shaped my zeal for following Jesus as
a young Dominican sister and assured me when I left the
convent that God could and would still use that zeal.*

*Last, but definitely not least, this book is dedicated
to my heavenly mother, Mary, whom Jesus gave
to me as model, guide, and mediatrix. Without
her "Yes," mine would be meaningless.*

Contents

Introduction

When I was a Dominican sister, I loved the time set aside before evening prayers for spiritual reading. I especially loved reading biographies of the saints. In their pages, I found inspiration and encouragement for living out my religious vocation.

It was not God's will, however, that I remain in the convent. So I came home, fell in love, got married, and began a family. I quickly realized two things: (1) I had very little time to read anything anymore, and (2) being a mommy was much harder than I expected.

I needed motivation and reassurance like I had received in the convent by reading about the saints. Then again, I wanted to find saints who experienced what I was experiencing. I longed to hear about women who had been there, done that, and survived motherhood. I wanted to read about saintly moms.

To my great delight, I found many canonized women, or

women on their way to canonization, who not only survived but thrived as mommies. That is not to say that motherhood was easy for them or that their lives were oh so wonderful. Not at all. The women you will meet within these pages are very human. Yet they used the graces given them to love and serve their families, neighbors, and God. They are my heroes. That's why I want to share their stories with you. Since I know you do not have a lot of free time, I tried to keep the chapters short enough for you to read before falling asleep, while in the car waiting to pick up your child, or whenever you can steal a few minutes for yourself. In each chapter of this book, I first tell the story of a saintly mom. Then I reflect on a lesson learned from her life. In the final section, I pray with you through the intercession of that holy mother. It is my hope that you will feel such a connection with some of these mommy saints that they will become your spiritual friends and inspiration.

We all can use some reassurance in this wonderful, crazy vocation of motherhood. Have no doubts about it, motherhood is a vocation. God has called you to be the mother of your children. With the gifts and virtues he has bestowed upon you, you are made to be a saint, and to help your husband and children become saints too.

So whether you are in the throes of motherhood or are enjoying the fruits of being a grandmother, whether you are raising children by yourself or have a wonderful, helpful husband, my hope is that within these pages you find encouragement and inspiration. My prayer is that you will be heartened by the saintly possibilities in your vocation. Become a saintly mom!

God bless you and your family.

Kelly Ann Guest

Blessed Mother Mary

FAST FACTS
c. 15 B.C.–A.D. 44

Major feast days: January 1, Mary, Mother of
God; March 25, the Annunciation; August 15, the
Assumption; December 8, the Immaculate Conception

Patron saint of all Christians

Children: One — Jesus Christ, Savior of the World

The greatest of all saints was a woman. A mother, as a matter of fact. Most of her life, she did what we do, day in and day out. Everything she did, she did for Jesus — literally. Mary is the role model for all of us who are moms.

By all outward appearances, Mary was an ordinary girl of her time. As a young teen, she was betrothed to Joseph, a modest and pious carpenter in her town of Nazareth. She was not yet living with Joseph when an extraordinary event happened — an event that would quietly change the world. The angel Gabriel was sent by God to ask Mary to become the mother of the Messiah. Moreover, it would be through the power of the Holy Spirit that she would conceive the Son of the Most High God. What trust in God Mary had to say yes to the Life that would grow within her womb! We, too, must trust in God's grace to support us when we become mommies.

When Mary gave her *fiat* to the angel, she became *the* Bearer of the Gospel and the very first apostle. An apostle is "one who is sent," and immediately she carried the Good News to her cousin Elizabeth in the town of Judah. Elizabeth, filled with the Holy Spirit, recognized right away that Mary was the mother of the Lord. In response, Our Lady gave praise to God: "My soul proclaims the greatness of the Lord; / my spirit rejoices in God my savior. / For he has looked upon his handmaid's lowliness; / behold, from now on will all ages call me blessed" (Lk 1:46–48). Mary gave praise to God for the high honor bestowed upon her. Motherhood increases humility in us, too. It is, therefore, only right and just to give God the praise for any good that we or our children accomplish.

Next Divine Providence led Mary and Joseph to King David's hometown, Bethlehem, for the Roman census. With all the rooms in the inns full, the King of kings was to be born, not in a castle, but a stable. Again, in all humility, Mary trusted that this was God's will. Because the newborn Savior of the World could be found in a manger and not a crowded inn, lowly shepherds could experience the Good News and share it with others. "All who heard it were amazed by what had been told them by the shepherds. And Mary kept all these things, reflecting on them in her heart" (Lk 2:18–19). Sometimes we do not understand what God is doing in our lives, but if we can be still and reflect upon God's ways, we can often begin to see his loving wisdom.

Forty days after Jesus' birth, Mary and Joseph took Jesus to the temple in Jerusalem in obedience to the law of Moses, which required every firstborn male to be dedicated to the Lord. Here, the hopes of two devout and faithful people, Simeon and Anna, were fulfilled. They beheld the Messiah! Joseph and Mary spread the hope of the Gospel simply by obeying the precepts their Jewish faith required of parents. Likewise, we as Christian parents are called to spread the hope that Jesus brings. By being faithful to the teachings of the Church, we can rest assured that we, too, will one day behold the glory of our Savior.

A newlywed couple was able to experience a part of Jesus' glory here on earth when, years later, as Jesus was beginning his public ministry, Mary shared the Good News with them at Cana. Seeing that they were running out of wine, an embarrassing situation for the nameless couple, Mary turned to her Son. Though not sure what exactly he would do, she trusted in his goodness and mercy. As in the case of this couple, Mary knew all married couples would need Jesus' help at times. So, in a gentle way, she urged Jesus to reveal his divinity at a wedding feast. "Do whatever he tells you" was her advice to the servers who would assist Jesus in this miracle (see Jn 2:5). These last words spoken by Mary in the Bible echo throughout time. Her advice to all of us is to trust him and do whatever he asks of us, especially in our marriages. Mary herself modeled this trust and did all that God asked of her, even when it was difficult.

She knew Jesus had a special mission from the Father, and

that he was the Messiah, the Savior of the World. The angel Gabriel had revealed this to her at the Annunciation. Mary knew Scripture and the prophecies regarding the Messiah. She had read and heard many times throughout her life the suffering servant songs of Isaiah and the twenty-second Psalm that prophesied the rejection and humiliation Jesus would endure. She had heard the prophecy of Simeon when she and Joseph presented Jesus in the temple. She knew the time would come when her mother's heart would be pierced. She did not fret about what was to come, but trusted that whatever this suffering would be, it, too, would bring about good because God is good.

So when that day arrived, the day we call Good Friday, she stood at the foot of the cross. Only a mother's heart can understand the suffering that Mary endured that day. The mother joined her sufferings with her Son's. Through Jesus' passion, her heartache became redemptive, too. Following the example of Our Lady, we can unite our sorrows with the sufferings of her Son. In this way, our sorrows can be redemptive and will not be in vain.

As Jesus' mission of salvation for all mankind was coming to an end, Mary accepted a new mission from her Son: He asked her to be the mother of his disciples, the mother of us all. In a very real way, Mary's work on earth was just beginning.

After Jesus' ascension, his mother remained with the apostles and prayed with them for the Holy Spirit to fill them as he had filled her. She continued to guide the young Church even after Pentecost. No doubt she reflected and shared her contemplations with Saint John. She also related stories to Saint Luke that he, in turn, wrote in his Gospel. Most of all, she prayed to her Son, and the Father and the Holy Spirit, praising God for the growth of the Church, asking for guidance for the apostles, requesting graces for the new believers, and trusting that God's will would be done.

Mary's mission as mother of the Savior of the World did not end with her assumption into heaven, either. After all, a mother's job is never done! To this day, she works to see that not a drop of her Son's blood is wasted. She continues to pray for our salvation. On occasion, God even sends Our Lady into the world to remind and encourage us. Mary continues to share the Good News with us, sending us the graces her Son won for us so that one day we may join them in heaven when our earthly mission here is completed.

HOLINESS IN EVERYDAY LIFE

Whether we are elbow deep in diapers, have all our children in school, or are empty nesters, most of our days are monotonous. Day after day, we have the same routine. Not much changes from one day to the next, but that is not necessarily a bad thing. There is something wonderful in our ordinary life. This is one of the many reasons I love the Blessed Mother so much. She was called to be the Mother of God. She experienced that extraordinary moment when she saw and talked to an angel! Then the angel left. And while in one way her life was never the same, at the same time her everyday life remained pretty ordinary. Most days, she just did the wife and mom thing: prepared meals, did chores, taught her child, helped neighbors. Yet she did it with great love and devotion.

The monotony of life was filled with joy because she did it with and for Jesus and Joseph. We, too, can experience joyful monotony when we do the ordinary tasks of everyday life with and for Jesus and our family. Because Mary performed these familial chores, they have been made holy. God has made the vocation of motherhood, in all its ordinariness, sanctifying.

For thirty years, Mary was simply Jesus' mom. Then, at the wedding feast of Cana, she did her part to reveal to us who he really is. She encouraged him to share his divinity with us. Life changed for both of them from that moment forward. Mary willingly gave Jesus to all of us.

We, in turn, must share Jesus with our families, co-workers, neighbors, and all who God places in our lives — especially our children. As mothers and apostles, we are sent to share the Good News that Jesus came to save us and sent the Holy Spirit to sanctify us. Furthermore, this truth gives joy and purpose to our every action.

In the typical routine of our everyday life, we can become saints. Our Lady shows us the way.

OUR PRAYER

Heavenly Father, we praise you for choosing a woman to have such an important role in your Son's salvific mission. Our roles may not be as great as Mary's, but they, too, are important. Help us, Lord, to do our part in bearing the Good News, first and foremost to our own families and then to all those whom you put into our lives. Through the intercession of the Blessed Virgin Mary, may our souls also proclaim your greatness, Lord. We ask this through her Son, Jesus Christ. Amen.

Saint Anne

FAST FACTS
First century B.C.

Feast day: July 26, shared with her
husband, Saint Joachim

Patron saint of grandmothers,
women in labor, and miners

Children: One — Mary

God can bring the best outcomes out of the worse situations. That is exactly what happened to Saints Anne and Joachim.

We do not know a whole lot about Jesus' grandparents. The important facts come to us from Tradition. I love that; after all, don't many of our own traditions come to us from our grandparents? How appropriate, then, that tradition plays a big part of what we know about Anne and Joachim.

In my retelling of their story, however, I fill in the gaps with the private revelations of Bl. Anne Catherine Emmerich and Ven. Mary of Jesus of Ágreda, as well as the *Protoevangelium of James*. The following is a mixture of these traditions, stories, and my imagination put together to recount the story of my beloved patron saint.

This I know for sure: Anne loved Joachim very much. Like his famous ancestor, King David, Joachim was said to be a successful shepherd. Being the generous, God-loving couple that they were, Anne and Joachim always gave one-third of their wealth to the poor — widows, orphans, and needy neighbors — and another third to the Lord through his temple in Jerusalem, while the remaining third supplied the couple with their needs. Those who knew them were aware of their charity. Yet a mystery surrounded this couple. For all their many blessings, they remained childless. Twenty years of a holy marriage had not produced the fruit of children. It was not through a lack of trying, nor through a lack of praying.

This was a source of sadness for Anne and Joachim for many years. Yet Anne learned to place her desire for a child fully in God's hands. Though she never stopped praying for a child, even if it seemed unlikely, Anne stopped letting her barren womb cause her grief. She knew the stories of Sarah and Hannah (her namesake) and how God gave them sons late in life. So, if God willed it, she would bear a child one day, too.

Nonetheless, Anne felt badly that her husband had to tolerate the constant whispering of neighbors and other shepherds behind his back. "Whose sin brought this curse upon the seemingly devout couple?" people wondered out loud.

Anne knew that it was not because of any sin that they could not conceive a child. She had come to realize that sometimes these things just are. For example, her sister Sobe's daughter, Elizabeth, had married a Levite living among the tribe of Judah a few years ago, and they, too, were still childless. Her sister, her niece, and her niece's husband were all good people. Sometimes, Anne concluded, for some unknown reason, God withheld his blessings.

One day, as he was accustomed to do, Joachim kissed Anne good-bye and headed to the temple in Jerusalem. He took with him the best lamb in his flock for a sacrifice. Anne knew Joachim deeply desired a son to help in the fields and to whom he could leave the fruits of his labors. Then again, a daughter would be wonderful, too. He and Anne had discussed the possibility of offering a daughter as a temple virgin. There, she would fulfill necessary tasks for the priests, like sewing vestments, washing liturgical linens, and weaving the temple veil. Holy women who were widowed would teach her these things and more — most importantly, how to read the Torah and participate in liturgical prayer. Either a son or a daughter would be a blessing.

Joachim usually returned from his trip to the temple after two or three days. This time, though, many days passed, and still her husband had not returned home. Anne began to worry. She prayed fervently for her husband's safe return. She inquired of neighbors, hoping someone knew of his whereabouts.

After many days and sleepless, prayer-filled nights, word got back to Anne. When Joachim had presented his lamb for sacrifice, the priest Reuben rejected him. He declared before those present that Joachim was sinful and unworthy to offer sacrifice before the Lord in his holy temple. Joachim was devastated. In his grief and embarrassment, he went into the hill country to fast and pray. There he planned to stay until God would lift the burden of his rejection.

When Anne heard this, she fell to her knees and prayed. She begged God for a child and promised that they would consecrate their child to the Lord's service. She cried out to the Lord in a way she had never done before, and God heard her cry.

An angel appeared to Anne. He told her she was already with child and that this child was indeed to be consecrated to the Lord. Her name was to be Mary, for out of their bitterness would come blessing. Truly, this child would be blessed through all generations.

The messenger of God also informed Anne that he had already delivered the good news to Joachim, who was on his way home. If she left immediately, she could meet him at the Golden Gate in Jerusalem. So Anne made haste to greet her husband. Upon reuniting at the Golden Gate, the holy couple embraced, and Anne, for the first time, felt the child within her move. Anne had always believed, but now she knew beyond all doubt that, with God, all things are possible. This is important for us to remember, too: Sometimes, God has already answered our prayers; we just don't know it yet.

A few months later, Anne gave birth to a beautiful baby girl. They named her Mary, as the angel had directed. Furthermore, the tradition tells us that Anne and Joachim kept their promise to the Lord. When Mary turned three, they took her to the temple in Jerusalem and consecrated her as a temple virgin. They left her in the hands of a widow named Anna. Mary would remain at the temple until she was about fourteen, when she would be dismissed to be married. For it was believed that there was a good chance that the Messiah would come from one of these temple virgins, fulfilling the prophecy of Isaiah: "Behold, the virgin shall be with child and bear a son, and they shall name him

Emmanuel" (Mt 1:23).

A quiet, righteous man named Joseph was chosen to become Mary's husband. Perhaps Anne and Joachim arranged their marriage, though some traditions say the High Priest chose Joseph for Mary. In any case, Mary was betrothed to a simple carpenter from Nazareth. Together with Jesus, they form the Holy Family.

REFLECTIONS OF OUR MOMS

For better or worse, our motherhood is an image of our own mother's. There are things that my mother said that I thought I would never say to my children. Things like "Because Y's a crooked letter and can't be straightened." (What does that even mean?) And "Eat it or wear it!" (which my grandmother said to my mother, so at least I am carrying on a tradition). I hope I also have some of my mother's good qualities: a giving heart, listening ears, and a persevering spirit. Our mothers shape us in more ways than one.

Though immaculately conceived and perfect, Mary was still formed by her mother. Saint Anne, by her example, showed Mary how to be a mother. Most statues and images of Saint Anne have Mary at her side with a book or scroll in her hand. What a beautiful reminder that, as mothers, we are the primary educators of our children. It is not an ABC book or a scroll of colors in Anne's hand, though. The book is too thick and the scroll too long. Anne is reading Scripture to Mary. Our utmost responsibility is to teach our children to know, love, and serve God. In the Rite of Baptism, the priest prays a blessing over the parents, saying they "will be the first teachers of their child in the ways of the Faith. May they be also the best of teachers, bearing witness to the faith by what they say and do, in Christ Jesus Our Lord." No doubt, Mary had the best of teachers.

You, too, are the best teacher for your children. Of all the possible parents God could have made for your child, he chose you. He knows you — all your faults and foibles, all your gifts and virtues. Likewise, he knows your child's needs and talents. God has known from all eternity that you are the perfect mom for this precious child of his. That is why he entrusted your child(ren) to you and your husband.

Saint Anne, however, is not the patron saint of mothers, but of grandmothers. Tradition does not tell us whether or not she ever got to see Jesus while on earth. Still, the Church recognizes the importance of grandmothers so much that she declares Jesus' own grandmother their patron. The traditions of faith, family, and love that a grandmother gives her family are invaluable and irreplaceable. A grandmother's affection is one of God's greatest gifts to a child. Moreover, becoming a grandmother is one of God's gifts to mothers who ultimately survive the blessing of motherhood.

So let your mom dote on your children. They both deserve it. And while you are at it, thank her for the example of motherhood she has given you.

OUR PRAYER

Heavenly Father, thank you for the gift of grandmothers. We praise you especially for the gift our mothers are to our children. Help us to imitate the good qualities of our mothers, while perfecting our own unique gifts of motherhood. Like Saint Anne, may we teach our children to love and trust you by our words and example. O Lord, through the intercession of Saint Anne, bless our mothers and grandmothers in time and eternity, through her Grandson, Jesus Christ. Amen.

Saint Elizabeth

FAST FACTS

First century B.C.–first century A.D.

Feast day: November 5

Patron saint of pregnant women

Children: One — St. John the Baptist

"Blessed are you among women, and blessed is the fruit of your womb" (Lk 1:42). These words from the Hail Mary were spoken for the first time by Saint Elizabeth. The mother of St. John the Baptist is one of the most important women in salvation history. Yet she spoke just three times in Scripture: when she discovered she was pregnant, when Mary visited her, and when she named her son John. All that we know about her is contained within the first chapter of Saint Luke's Gospel.

Elizabeth and her husband Zechariah were described as righteous and blameless before the Lord (see Lk 1:6). Luke also uses one other word, however, to describe this godly woman: barren (v. 7). Like a wasteland, her womb was seemingly lifeless. She and her husband Zechariah had no children, and they "were advanced in years."

One year Zechariah, being of Israel's Levitical priesthood, traveled to the temple in Jerusalem to perform his priestly duties. By chance, Zechariah was chosen for a once-in-a-lifetime opportunity: to burn incense and offer prayers in the temple's second holiest chamber, the Holy Place. In the outer chamber, the people offered their sacrifices and prayed evening prayer, then awaited Zechariah's blessing after he exited the inner chamber. The animal sacrifices were consumed by the holy fire; the prayers were recited. The people waited and waited. What happened to Zechariah? They began to worry.

Inside the Holy Place, the angel Gabriel appeared to Zechariah. The angel declared that Zechariah's prayer was heard; Elizabeth would bear a son! And not just any son, for his son would be the forebearer of the Messiah, preparing the way of the Lord. Zechariah just could not believe it, and in his heart he questioned how it could be. "How shall I know this? For I am an old man, and my wife is advanced in years" (Lk 1:18). He was asking for a sign, and Gabriel gave him one: "Now you will be speechless and unable to talk until the day these things take place, because you did not believe my words" (Lk 1:20). When Zechariah finally exited the chamber mute, the people realized he had seen a vision.

I wonder how Zechariah explained to Elizabeth when he got home all that had happened in Jerusalem. Maybe by signs, or perhaps by writing. In any case, Elizabeth believed her husband, and she trusted that God would fulfill his promise.

Elizabeth did indeed conceive a child, despite her advanced age. What did she do when she realized that her days of being barren were over? Did she jump up and down for joy? No, after all, she was quite old (some scholars believe she may have even been in her eighties!). Did she go to gloat at the well where all the women hung out? I would have, but not Elizabeth. She went into seclusion.

Some suggest that Elizabeth hid because she was embarrassed. I do not think so, for when she realized she was pregnant, she spoke her first recorded words in Scripture, proclaiming, "So the Lord has done for me at a time when he has seen fit to take away my disgrace before others" (Lk 1:25). Her pregnancy was a source of grace, not humiliation.

Elizabeth knew that this child was going to be special. God had a mission for him. Aware of her advanced years, perhaps she put herself on a type of bedrest. She wanted to protect what God had entrusted to her. So she spent this time in prayer and thanksgiving. With anticipation, Elizabeth prepared for her son's arrival.

After five months of self-imposed quarantine, Elizabeth received a visit from her young cousin, Mary. Right away Elizabeth knew that the mother of her Lord had come to visit her. Mary brought divine grace to Elizabeth and her unborn child. From within his mother's womb, Jesus delivered John from original sin, and John, in his mother's womb, leaped for joy. The angel Gabriel's prophecy that John would be "filled with the holy Spirit even from his mother's womb" was fulfilled (Lk 1:15). It was then that Elizabeth proclaimed those words that we pray in the Hail Mary: "Blessed are you among women, and blessed is the fruit of your womb" (v. 42).

For three months, Mary stayed with Elizabeth. On the practical side, Mary helped Elizabeth with household chores during the exhausting third trimester of her pregnancy. They bolstered one another as they compared stories, shared concerns, and gave glory to God for his goodness to them and to the world by sending the Savior. Surely, they prayed together, laying before the Almighty God their petitions and thanksgiving. The bond formed from their common experience encouraged both women.

Eight days after Elizabeth's baby was born, he was circumcised and given his name. Family and friends who were there to join the celebration were surprised when Elizabeth declared that his name was to be John. Clearly this firstborn son, so long awaited by both parents, ought to be named after his father. So they turned to Zechariah to confirm the child's name. Motioning for a tablet, the father, in obedience to the angel's message, wrote, "John is his name" (Lk 1:63). At once, Zechariah was able to speak again and immediately gave praise to God. Thus, Elizabeth and Zechariah worked together to fulfill God's will.

Elizabeth is not mentioned in the Bible after John's circumcision. Many years later, however, Jesus stated, "Amen, I say to you, among those born of women there has been none greater than John the Baptist" (Mt 11:11). Saint Elizabeth raised her son to be the man God called him to be. God has a special calling for each of our children. May he grant us the graces to raise them to recognize their calling, like Saint Elizabeth did for John.

THE TRIALS OF INFERTILITY

Infertility is a heavy cross to carry. It is also a great mystery. Why was I able to conceive so easily and give birth to nine healthy children when other wonderful women are unable to have any children at all?

I have friends and family who are infertile, never having any children of their own. These beautiful women find joy in nieces and nephews, neighborhood children, and foster children. They embrace a spiritual motherhood. I also have friends who have adopted and given abundant love and happy homes to beautiful children. A local minister and his wife adopted eight incredible children with various physical disabilities. Another couple adopted a boy from Russia and, soon after they brought their son home, discovered they were expecting! God calls some parents to accept into their hearts and homes children who need a loving family.

My husband's godmother was infertile for twenty-two years. Resigning herself to God's will, she started a ministry to help pregnant teens. Then, for her fortieth birthday, God opened her womb to beautiful twin girls! She, like Elizabeth, marveled that "at a time when he has seen fit," God fulfilled her dream to have children.

There are women who dream of having large families. God blesses them with one, maybe two children, then they are unable to have any more. This, too, is a type of infertility, which is the cause of suffering and resignation to God's design.

Saint Elizabeth knew the heartache of being infertile. She experienced the discouragement, felt the heartache, and ignored the thoughtless comments. Even when she did not understand, Elizabeth still trusted and loved the Lord.

Love is the vocation of every mother, whether one is called to physical or spiritual motherhood. God asks that we nurture the children he has placed in our lives. As women of faith, we point these children to Jesus and, like John the Baptist, declare, "Behold, the Lamb of God" (Jn 1:36).

OUR PRAYER

Father, Creator of all life, we praise you for the gift of children. Thank you for the delight they bring to the world. Through the intercession of Saint Elizabeth, bless the wombs of all women who desire children. May they and their husbands experience the joy of raising children for your glory. For those who cannot bear children, Father, we ask that they find peace and happiness in a spiritual motherhood that truly benefits the world. May we always rejoice in all that you have given us, through Christ, Our Lord. Amen.

Saint Perpetua

FAST FACTS
c. A.D. 182–203

Feast day: March 7

Patron saint of expectant mothers,
ranchers, and butchers

Children: One — An unnamed son

Have you ever met a woman who seems to have everything — beauty, intelligence, wealth, a good-looking husband, and beautiful children? Perpetua, a young noblewoman from second-century Carthage, was one of those women. What more could she possibly need or want? Faith. Faith like her mother's. The Christian faith.

The child of a pagan father and a Christian mother living in a pagan world, Perpetua, at the age of twenty-two, decided to become a catechumen. Her servant girl, Felicity, and two men joined Saturus, a respected catechist, for instruction in the Christian Faith. Eager to grow in their faith, these young people often met on their own to "seek what is above" (Col 3:1). During one of these meetings, the four catechumens were arrested. Not wanting his pupils to suffer alone and desiring to encourage them, Saturus turned himself in to the authorities as well. At first, the small group was placed under house arrest until a trial could be held. Here, the catechumens were baptized. After their baptism of water and the Spirit, their desire to shed their blood for Christ grew fervently.

While on house arrest, Perpetua and the others were frequently allowed visitors. Her mother, brother, and father would bring her infant son to her. Perpetua's greatest concern was her son's health and nutrition. She was greatly relieved, in mind and body, to be able to nurse her child.

After her trial, where she refused to sacrifice to the Roman gods and declared herself to be a Christian, Perpetua was thrown with the others into prison. The conditions were horrible. The cells were overcrowded, excessively hot, and totally dark. Worst of all was being separated from her son. The saint began to languish from the anxiety of separation. The deacons who ministered to the prisoners paid the jailer to move Perpetua so that she would be able to keep her infant son with her. Together, she and her son began to grow stronger. With her son in her arms, the dungeon became a palace to her.

While Perpetua was imprisoned, God communicated with her on multiple occasions. First, after her baptism, he told her to pray for endurance during her trial. When her brother asked her to pray to God and ask him whether this trial would end with release or in martyrdom, Perpetua had a vision in which she ascended a ladder fixed with all kinds of weapons and a crouching dragon lying in wait under it. At the top of the ladder, she was welcomed to an immense garden by a shepherd of large stature and thousands of white-robed people. She was also given two other visions, both about her young brother who had died years before of a flesh-eating cancer. In the first vision, she saw him with repugnant wounds on his face, struggling and unable to get a drink from a pool of water. Disturbed by this vision, she prayed in earnest for her brother and offered her sufferings for his soul. Days later, she again saw her brother, but this time with a clean body. He was able to draw water from the pool and drank it from a golden goblet, before going off joyfully to play. Perpetua understood that her brother had been released from purgatory and was enjoying the rewards of eternal life. Her heart was full of peace, knowing that she would soon be reunited with her little brother. God's communications consoled Perpetua in the face of her impending martyrdom.

On the day of their martyrdom, Perpetua, Felicity, and their companions walked into the amphitheater as if they were going to a marriage feast. The men were placed first in the exhibition. Bears and wild boars killed them all, except Saturus. He had had a dream the night before which revealed that he would achieve his glory through the bite of a leopard. So it did not surprise him when the bear refused to do him harm, and they had to bring out the big cat. Next, Perpetua and Felicity were placed in the arena with a rabid heifer. Though they were tossed around and bloodied, they were not killed. The crowd, tired of the games, cried out, "Enough!" They just wanted the Christians dead. Now faced with gladiators, the two young mothers were killed by the sword. In Saturus's dream before his death, he had seen Perpetua in her glory. She spoke to him: "Joyous as I was in the flesh, I am now more joyous here." For all the wonderful things she had in this life, Perpetua knew the one thing that mattered most was faith in Jesus Christ. She was willing to give up her earthly life, including her young son, for eternal life.

Perpetua was able to wean her baby boy before her death and entrusted his care to her mother. She knew that God would keep him in his loving care. Before the face of God, she would continue to pray for her son, her husband, her father (who was not Christian and mourned her terribly), her family, and friends. From heaven, Perpetua could provide for her child and loved ones in ways beyond our understanding.

****

Some early saints have had legends built up around them so that we can no longer be sure what is truth, exaggerated fact, or just plain ol' fiction. This is not the case with Saint Perpetua. She kept a journal while in prison. The *Passion of Saint Perpetua, Saint Felicitas and Their Companions*, one of the oldest Christian history books, contains her diary as well as an eyewitness account of the actual martyrdom. What we know about Saint Perpetua today we are assured of by her own words.

In her own writing, we have the story of how committed to Christ she was. When her father came to her while she was in prison, she tells how he actually got on his knees and begged her for love of her infant son and out of affection for him to offer sacrifice to the pagan gods so that she could go free. She then pointed to a water jug and asked her father: "'Do you see this vase here, for example, or waterpot or whatever?' 'Yes, I do,' said he. And I told him: 'Could it be called by any other name than what it is?' And he said: 'No.' 'Well, so too I cannot be called anything other than what I am, a Christian.'"

No doubt, Perpetua loved her father and her son very much, but she loved God even more.

APPRECIATING THE MOMENT

As moms, we ought to cherish each phase of motherhood that we are experiencing. Saint Perpetua enjoyed every moment spent with her boy. True, it is unrealistic to think we will actually enjoy every moment we spend with our children. There are times that are difficult and frustrating. Still, the lesson I learned from Saint Perpetua is to appreciate the moment I am in right now.

Nursing a baby is a bonding experience. Like Saint Perpetua, I appreciated the time to be able to sit quietly and rest with my child. But not always. If I am honest, often I was thinking about all that I had to get done and wishing the baby would hurry up! What a shame to miss the moment. Though at the time it may seem to never end, or at least not end fast enough, those moments truly do not last long.

Every phase of childhood brings joys and difficulties in motherhood. There will be trials and triumphs. Waking up to feed a newborn every other hour is exhausting, but eventually your child will sleep through the night. Then childhood nightmares will have you scrambling to a bedside or finding a little one snuggling against you in your bed for comfort and reassurance. These moments give way to you sitting up until their curfew to be assured that your teen arrives home safely.

We go from running after them, to running them around, to worrying about where they are running to now. When they're little, we can make their boo-boos all better with a kiss and a Band-aid®, but as they get older, we can only pray for broken hearts to be healed. In no time, pushing them in carts down grocery aisles turns into watching them walk down the aisle of the church. The days may go by slowly, but the years fly by. So hang on to the moment you are in.

Saint Perpetua did not get to enjoy all these different phases with her son, yet she treasured the time she had with him. Ultimately, our time with our children is short. In difficult moments, take a deep breath and say a little prayer. Ask God what he is trying to teach you in this moment — what is he asking of you right now? We grow spiritually as our children grow physically.

Savor the good days and precious moments. They are fleeting, too. The one constant is our love for our children. Like Saint Perpetua, "we look not to what is seen but to what is unseen; for what is seen is transitory, but what is unseen is eternal" (2 Cor 4:18). Whatever phase, whatever circumstance you find yourself in, continue on in love.

OUR PRAYER

Heavenly Father, all praise and glory be to you for the courage, strength, and witness of your martyrs. Help us to die to self in the many little ways that motherhood offers us. Help us to appreciate the phase of motherhood that we are in right now. Through the intercession of Saint Perpetua, may our love and devotion to family be second only to our love and devotion to you. We ask this through Jesus Christ, Our Lord. Amen.

Saint Bassa

FAST FACTS
Third century, died A.D. 304

Feast day: August 21

Children: Three — Saints Theogonius,
Agapius, and Fidelis

The death of a child, whether it be through a miscarriage, after an illness, or because of a tragic accident, is a heavy sorrow for parents to bear. Only the hope of a heavenly reunion can give them peace amid such heartbreak. It was this hope that enabled Saint Bassa to witness the death of her three sons — that and a heck of a lot of graces!

Saint Bassa was a Christian in Syria during the rule of the Roman Emperor Diocletian. Her husband, on the other hand, was a pagan priest. He worshipped Zeus above all, but depending on the situation, he would make sacrifices to one of the many other Greek gods or demigods. Bassa and her sons Theogonius, Agapius, and Fidelis, however, always prayed in the name of Jesus Christ, and the Eucharist was the only sacrifice in which they partook.

Now, Saint Bassa stood before the governor of Edessa, with her three sons bound beside her as prisoners. They had been arrested for being Christian. Their accuser was her husband, the father of the boys.

Bassa was made to watch the martyrdom of each son in hopes of eventually breaking her, causing her to deny her faith. Each young man was given a chance to offer sacrifices to idols. One by one, they refused.

As the boys were tortured, their mother fortified them: "Be brave, my sons, and remain loyal to the one true God." How could a mother just stand there and say this? Saint Bassa was filled with holy wisdom that assured her of the true life awaiting her sons. The pain, agonizing as it was, would last but a short time; the reward would be eternal.

First, Bassa witnessed her eldest son, Theogonius, suspended by his wrists and ankles. As he continued to repudiate their false gods, the officials struck him with irons until his flesh was completely torn.

Her middle son, Agapius, was flayed, skinned alive, before

Bassa's eyes.

The youngest, Fidelis, was beheaded.

Though she was brokenhearted, Bassa's faith remained unbroken. She would rely on the grace of God to get her through until she saw her boys again in Paradise.

After her sons' martyrdoms, Bassa was thrown in prison. Wishing to weaken her, the authorities did not feed her. Legend says that an angel was sent to strengthen her with heavenly food.

Her guards tried to torture her by fire, but she was untouched by the flames. She was thrown into an arena with wild beasts, yet remained unharmed. God was manifesting his saving power.

One final time, she was brought into the pagan temple to offer sacrifice in exchange for her freedom. As she entered the temple, the statue of Zeus shattered.

Saint Bassa was thrown back into prison until the authorities could figure out what to do with her. When a whirlpool was spotted in the sea, they decided to throw her into the water to be swallowed up by the ocean. Once again, Bassa was saved as a ship sailed up to her and three radiant young men pulled her aboard. It is believed that the men were her sainted sons.

After sailing for eight days, Bassa came to the end of her journey. She disembarked on the island of Alona in the Sea of Marmora (near Istanbul, Turkey). There, the authorities had Bassa beaten with rods and finally beheaded.

It is hard to say how much of what we know of Bassa is fact and how much is legend. We do know that Saint Bassa was made to witness the martyrdom of her sons, and that she, too, was eventually martyred. We can also be assured that the mother and her boys are now enjoying the fruits of their faithfulness.

THE LOSS OF A CHILD

A mother experiences sorrow beyond words when she loses a child. A child's death is devasting and heart-wrenching. Saint

Bassa watched all three of her sons die in the most horrific ways. Only through the grace of God could she persevere and remain strong in her faith.

On a smaller scale, I experienced this grace when I miscarried my son, Thomas Gabriel. God sent me comfort through a Bible verse: "You also are now in anguish. But I will see you again, and your hearts will rejoice, and no one will take your joy away from you" (Jn 16:22). This was actually the Gospel reading on the day of my D&C procedure. I know that in this reading Jesus was speaking to his disciples, but on that day, it was as if the Lord was allowing Thomas to speak to me. At a time when I was inconsolable, God found a way to console me.

The loss of Thomas brought home to me the truth that ultimately our children belong to God. As parents, we cooperate in God's creative plan to bring our children into this world. Parents provide the physical body of a child, but only God can create a soul. When we have our child baptized, God animates that soul with his very own Spirit. The gift God has given us, we give back to him. Our child is now a child of God, destined for everlasting life with him in heaven.

Every day with our children is a gift — even the exhausting and frustrating days. Our time with them on this earth is limited. Yet heaven is timeless. We are all God's children on our way home to him. Saint Bassa understood this truth. So, while it was excruciatingly difficult to watch her sons die, she had the reassurance that it was not the end of their lives. The hope of heaven makes the death of a loved one, especially a child, bearable.

For us mommies who have lost children, there will always be a hole in our hearts. God, however, can and will fill that hole with his peace and strength. Time will ease the intensity of the pain caused by the loss. Eventually, memories become a source of joy, and we can thank God for the time he gave us with our child. Joyfully, we await the blessed reunion in heaven.

OUR PRAYER

Father in heaven, thank you for the gift of our children. Help us to raise them to know, love, and serve you so that their lives may glorify you. They belong to you, not us, Lord. We pray especially for those who are grieving the loss of a child. Through the intercession of Saint Bassa, fill them with your strength, peace, and love. You promise to be close to the brokenhearted and save the crushed in spirit (Ps 34:19). Help these parents to feel your presence and be comforted. May the Blessed Mother, who has experienced this same pain, be ever near to them. We ask this through her Son, Our Lord, Jesus Christ. Amen.

Saint Helen

FAST FACTS
c. 248–c. 328

Feast day: August 18 in the Roman rite; May 21 in
the Eastern calendar (along with Saint Constantine)

Patron saint of archaeologists, converts,
divorced, and empresses

Children: One — Constantine the Great

From a young age, I wanted to be a missionary. I even took five years of Spanish in high school just in case God called me to the mission fields. Today I am a mom of nine and, indeed, a missionary. My mission field is my home. I see my mission in the eyes of each one of my children. I am a mom with a mission.

Saint Helen was a mom with a mission, too. When her son, Constantine the Great, became Augustus, or emperor, of the Roman Empire, he appointed his mother Augusta Imperatrix and tasked her with locating and preserving sacred objects and holy relics from the Holy Land. Though she was in her sixties, Helen undertook this mission with great enthusiasm and energy — quite astonishing considering she was not born a Christian.

Helen was born in Asia Minor, the daughter of Greek innkeepers of modest means. She herself was said to have been the stable maid at her father's inn. When General Constantius Chlorus stayed at the inn while stationed in Asia Minor, he fell in love with the humble maid and married her. Soon thereafter, she bore him a son, whom they named Flavius Valerius Constantinus, called Constantine, after his father.

When Constantius became Caesar in 293, he divorced his wife of low status to marry Theodora, the daughter of Emperor Maximian. Helen and her son were, therefore, ousted to the court of Diocletian. There, both mother and son witnessed the terrible persecution of Christians. During this time, Helen lived in relative obscurity while her son rose in the ranks of Rome's inner circle.

Upon the death of his father, Constantine was acclaimed emperor of the western provinces — what is now England, Spain, Portugal, and France. Both Constantine and his mother returned to the imperial court.

Though he was not yet a Christian, one of Constantine's first official acts was to sign the Edict of Milan, which ended the persecution of Christians and allowed them to practice their religion freely. Helen, who had been edified by the courage and charity of the Christians, soon became a Christian herself.

With great zeal, she began living her faith. She wore simple clothing, attended Mass as often as she could, visited and financially supported churches throughout Rome, and assisted the poor and imprisoned. Helen became a model of Christian living.

Meanwhile, Constantine's power spread throughout the whole Roman Empire. During this time, the Emperor sent his mother to the Holy Land. Jerusalem was still in the midst of rebuilding after its total destruction by Titus in A.D. 70. Furthermore, in 135, Hadrian had built a temple to Venus and Jupiter over the site of Jesus' burial. First, Helen had the temple destroyed and the site excavated in hopes of uncovering Jesus' tomb. Indeed, the Holy Sepulcher was unearthed. Not far from the burial site, three crosses, four nails, and some rope, as well as part of the sign Pilate had hung above Jesus' head on the cross, were also discovered. Knowing that the precious cross on which hung our Savior had to be one of those three, Helen sent for a sick woman who was near death. When the invalid touched the true cross of Christ, she was immediately healed. Thus, Saint Helen is credited with finding the most sacred relic in all the Church.

Constantine ordered a church to be built on the site of Jesus' death and resurrection, covering the area from Golgotha to the Tomb. It took ten years for the magnificent Church of the Holy Sepulcher to be built; Helen never saw its completion. She did, however, erect churches in Bethlehem where Jesus was born, and on the Mount of Olives where he ascended into heaven.

Saint Helen spent the last years of her life in the Holy Land. Along with building churches there, she supported the poor and suffering, especially prisoners, wounded soldiers, and mine workers. Though an empress, she humbly served pilgrims, washing their hands and feet and feeding them at her table. This mom with a mission put her whole heart into what was asked of her.

Through Saint Helen's influence, Christianity spread. Finding the relics of the passion of Christ increased devotion within the Church, and still does today. Her discoveries, though, are not what made her a saint. Saint Helen followed in Christ's footsteps of humble service to others. That is why she is a saint.

OUR MISSION AS MOMS

We are all moms with a mission. God has tasked us with work that no one else can complete. Within the workplace and in our homes, we influence and touch people's lives in a way no one else can. That is why God put these people in our lives.

Our day-to-day work may not seem glamorous or heroic, but it is important work. God has entrusted our children to us. We are to take care of them and teach them about God. From going grocery shopping to going to church as a family, we are carrying out the work God has given to us. Moreover, we show our children by our example how to love and serve God. When we take food to a sick neighbor, volunteer at church, or participate in clothing or canned good drives at school and church, we demonstrate our faith in action. Beginning at home, mothers mirror God's love.

Outside the home, we also give witness to our faith. We act as missionaries in the workplace when we are kind to coworkers, even the most difficult ones. When we guard our speech, we preach without using words. We work hard not so much for that raise or promotion, but because this is the work God has provided for us. We do it for his glory.

We may not build magnificent churches, like Saint Helen did, yet we are walking temples of the Holy Spirit. We may never touch the true cross of Christ, but we can help others carry their crosses. We may never see the sign that declared "Jesus of Nazareth, King of the Jews," but we can be a sign to others that Jesus is truly King and Lord of our lives. This is our mission!

OUR PRAYER

Heavenly Father, we praise you for the unique gifts you have given each one of us. Thank you for calling us to serve you through those you put into our lives. May we, through the intercession of Saint Helen, accomplish the special mission you have given us. We ask this through your Son, who lives and reigns with you and the Holy Spirit, one God forever. Amen.

Saint Monica

FAST FACTS
332–387

Feast day: August 27

Patron saint of married women and mothers

Children: Three — Saint Augustine,
Navigius, and Perpetua

Our children come back from college different from when they left our homes after high school. Most of the time, they are more mature, more independent, and ready to take on the world. Unfortunately, many lose their faith and desire to practice their religion once they leave home. As parents, we will always love our children; nonetheless, their rejection of the faith in which we baptized and raised them is heartbreaking. We need to pray persistently for their return to the Church, as Saint Monica did for her son Augustine. She sent her son away to school, and he came back believing a heresy!

Augustine was seventeen years old when his father died. His parents' marriage had been a rocky one. Monica's husband, Patricius, had a violent temper and was a womanizer. To make matters even more trying, Monica's cantankerous mother-in-law lived with them. Patricius, being a pagan, would not allow Monica to have their children baptized. Furthermore, he often ridiculed Monica's charity and piety. Yet Monica bore all this with gentleness and patience.

Monica prayed unceasingly for her husband's conversion. Her prayers were eventually answered when, a year before his death, he was baptized. Patricius admitted that, although he made fun of her faith, he truly admired her. Monica's sacrificial love had won her husband over to the Faith.

Years of observing his abusive father had their effect on their oldest son, Augustine. He was lazy, uncouth, and wild. After Patricius' death, Monica decided to send the intelligent young man away to Carthage for school. Her hope was that a proper education would straighten him out.

On a visit home, Augustine was proudly sharing with his mother his newfound knowledge. Not long into the discussion, she realized that he had fallen for the errors of the Manichaean heresy. In tears, Monica drove her firstborn away from her home.

Monica now had a new intention for which to pray and fast: and she did so with many tears. During prayer one day, Monica was weeping over her son's behavior when a mysterious figure appeared to her and asked why she was crying so. Then he told her to dry her tears, for "your son is with you." Comforted and confident, Monica set out to reconcile with Augustine.

Her vision would not be realized for many more years, though. Monica continued to pray and fast. Augustine, meanwhile, at the age of twenty-nine, took a mistress and had a son. He decided to move to Rome, quite possibly to get away from his mother. Monica had expressed a desire to go with him, so he lied to her about the time his ship was leaving. Not to be discouraged, the ever-persistent mother boarded the next ship to Rome.

When she arrived, Monica sought out her son, only to discover that he had left for Milan. In Milan, the faithful matriarch at last found her elusive son. To her delight, she discovered that Augustine was under the influence of the bishop of Milan, Ambrose, whose ability to explain the Faith mesmerized the scholar. Between his mother's prayers and sacrifices and Saint Ambrose's preaching and teaching, Augustine finally accepted and embraced the Catholic Faith.

After six months of pure joy and peace, Monica and Augustine decided to go back home to Tagaste, Africa, to spread the Faith. While waiting at the port in Ostia, Italy, Monica fell ill. For nine days, she suffered while Augustine and his brother, Navigius, prayed for her. With her job here on earth completed, God took her home to heaven. From there, she would continue to pray for her children and all the good God would work through them until their jobs on earth were done.

****

Saint Monica is also sometimes invoked as a patron of alcoholics.

This practice came about because of a story from her childhood.

When she was young, Monica was often given the task of fetching wine from the cellar for her family. Often, Monica would sneak a sip. Eventually, she developed a taste for the alcoholic beverage and would visit the wine cellar even when she was not sent. Monica was becoming an alcoholic.

Then, one day, a servant spied the young girl sneaking to the wine cellar and followed her. When confronted, Monica was so embarrassed that she never touched the drink again. We can, therefore, pray to Saint Monica not only for those who have wandered from the Faith but also for those who have become addicted to alcohol.

PERSISTING IN PRAYER

We pray for an intention for a week, a month, a year, or more, and our request may go unheeded — so we think. After some time, we may even give up praying for that intention. Monica teaches us an important lesson, especially as we pray for our spouse and children: Don't quit!

Jesus makes it clear that we are to be persistent in our prayer (see Lk 11:5–10 and 18:1–8). As mothers especially, we are called to follow the example of Saint Monica. She prayed, fasted, and shed tears for her son for more than *sixteen* years. Sometimes she wavered and had to be bolstered by others. For instance, Saint Ambrose had to assure the mother that "the child of so many tears can never be lost." On another occasion, the bishop advised her to "talk to your son less about God and more to God about your son." Thus, she continued praying and fasting. She didn't give up. In the end, her prayers and sacrifices paid off.

Certain prayer intentions are so pleasing to God that he always desires to grant them — the conversion of a child, spouse, or anyone dear to you is among these. You may need to add fasting and sacrifice to your prayer for the more stubborn-hearted to be touched, but never despair. God can reach them.

One of the greatest gifts, however, that God has given us is our free will. With it, we can choose to believe in God or not. He does not make us love and serve him. Our Creator respects our freedom. Still, God has ways of turning hearts toward him: "I will give you a new heart, and a new spirit I will put within you. I will remove the heart of stone from your flesh and give you a heart of flesh" (Ez 36:26). With our prayers and sacrifices, he can bring about the conversion of a loved one.

It may take some time. Like heart surgery, conversion is delicate work. Do not become discouraged in your prayer. "The Lord does not delay his promise, as some regard 'delay,' but he is patient with you, not wishing that any should perish but that all should come to repentance" (2 Pt 3:9). So surrender your child to him. Then, "be still before the LORD; / wait for him" (Ps 37:7). God is worthy of our trust. He will not disappoint. Saint Monica and Saint Augustine are proof of that.

OUR PRAYER

Heavenly Father, we praise you for your faithfulness. Thank you for always answering our prayers. We commend to you our children; may they always do your will and follow your Son. When they wander, bring them back into the fold. Through the intercession of Saint Monica, may we always trust in your promise that not one of them will be lost. We ask this through your Son, Jesus Christ, the Good Shepherd. Amen.

Saint Gladys

FAST FACTS
Late fifth to early sixth century

Feast day: March 29

Patron saint of Newport, Wales

Children: Seven — Saint Cadoc, Cynidr, Bugi,
Cyfyw, Maches, Gluvias, and Egwine

I know many mini-Monicas — women who are fervently praying for wayward children to come back to the Church. It's not as often that I encounter children praying for their mothers' conversions. Yet, it happens. Saint Gladys, for example, was converted by her son, Cadoc.

Gladys was the eldest daughter of Welsh king Brychan. She was so beautiful that she caught the eye of the neighboring king, Gwynllyw Farfog, also known as King Woolos. He asked King Brychan for his daughter's hand in marriage; however, since Woolos was not a Christian, Brychan refused. No matter to Woolos — he gathered three hundred of his men and kidnapped the princess!

Clearly, Woolos was a rough, uncouth chieftain, rather than a civilized, peaceful ruler. Yet following the classic story line of a good girl falling for the bad guy, Gladys happily married Woolos.

Their marriage was not one of mutual sanctification. On the contrary, Gladys abandoned her Christian upbringing and embraced her husband's brigand ways. Together they conducted a life of piracy. A sort of pre-Bonnie and Clyde, they lived life on the run.

One day, during one of their cattle-rustling adventures, Woolos and Gladys stole the only cow of a holy hermit, Tatheus. The courageous monk confronted the couple. They had already slaughtered the cow, so they could not give it back. Instead, they gave him their firstborn son, Cadoc. Don't be aghast — it was not uncommon in their day for parents to entrust their children to monks to be educated, as there were few to no schools in the fifth century. The nerve of the audacious monk impressed the king, and Tatheus saw an opportunity to influence the prince in a positive way.

Under the guidance of Saint Tatheus, Cadoc did, indeed, grow to be a saintly young man. He recognized the perils of his parents' lifestyle and prayed fervently for their conversion, as well as for his siblings. He had long conversations with his mother when she came to visit. Eventually, he was able to bring forth the graces of her baptism. Gladys began to realize the errors of her ways.

The queen then began to work on her husband. "Let us trust our son," Gladys told Woolos, "and he will be a father to us in heaven." Not until after a dream, however, did the king become Christian. In his vision, he was told to look for a white ox on Stow Hill. A white ox — was there really such an animal? When he actually spied the white ox on the exact hill where he was told, Woolos converted.

Both Gladys and Woolos confessed their sins and did penance in expiation of their crimes. Among other things, they ate a vegetarian diet (I guess to make up for the many cows they had stolen); they built churches and monasteries, including the one that still stands today on Stow Hill in Newport, South Wales; and they performed many charitable works. They turned out to be just and peaceful monarchs.

After several years of ruling his kingdom well, Woolos gave up his kingship and retired to a small retreat house. Gladys went, too. There they lived a life of mutual sanctification, fasting, and prayer. Gladys would bathe in the icy waters of the River Usk. As they grew in holiness, they stored up treasures in heaven.

Shortly before his death, Woolos moved into Cadoc's abbey. Gladys lived in a hermitage nearby. She spent the rest of her life drawing closer to the Lord she had neglected for so many years. The violent days of her youth turned into peaceful years in her maturity.

Saint Gladys got lost for a while. She got caught up in this life, pursuing what she thought was fun and exciting. Yet through the prayers and sacrifices of her son, Gladys found her way back home to the Faith into which she had been baptized. Furthermore, she became a saint! Her husband, Saint Gwynllyw, and son Saint Cadoc, and some of her other children, are also canonized saints. Let us never doubt the power of prayer and sacrifices.

LEARNING FROM OUR CHILDREN

As parents, we have the awesome responsibility to teach our children. Yet, as any good teacher will admit, our children can also teach us much.

Sometimes, they ask questions that require us to really think or search out the answer, like "Why are you crying if you are happy?" "Can ants swim?" and the one I still do not really get myself, "Why is the sky blue?" The questions of a toddler are wonderfully exhausting. The questions of teenagers are fewer yet more complex. Wisdom is a very helpful virtue for a parent.

Then again, there are times when children are so observant and innocent that they can correct us, as Cadoc did his parents. I personally have heard from the lips of babes, "Mommy, you shouldn't say that" and "You and daddy just need to kiss and make up." Humility is another necessary virtue for a parent.

Best of all is when we learn by just watching our children grow and mature. For instance, I have learned from my son that if you desire something good, tell God exactly what you hope for, and trust him to give it. God will indeed provide. From my daughter, who suffers from depression, I have learned that shining for others is possible even when all you feel is darkness. Best of all, each one of my children has shown me unconditional love. While pride is not a virtue, it is, nonetheless, a blessing to be proud of your children.

My children inspire me. They help me to grow as a parent and a person. In so many ways, it is because of them that I can become a saint.

OUR PRAYER

Heavenly Father, we praise you for the wonder of our children and the many talents you have given them. We ask that you help them to always use their talents for your glory. Through the intercession of Saint Gladys, may our children be an inspiration, not only to us, their parents, but also to all those who encounter them. We ask this through Our Lord and Savior Jesus Christ. Amen.

Saint Theneva

FAST FACTS
510–570

Feast day: July 18

Patron saint of Glasgow, Scotland

Children: Six — Saint Kentigern, Lleuddad,
Baglan, Eleri, Tygwy, and Tyfriog

When faced with an unplanned pregnancy, a woman's life can turn topsy-turvy pretty quickly. A mother in such a situation needs lots of love, support, and a bit of wisdom. This is what Saint Theneva found when, at eight months pregnant, her path literally crossed Saint Serf's.

When the maiden princess Theneva was found to be pregnant, her angry father sentenced her to death. To the pagan King Lleuddun (Loth), it did not matter that the child was conceived through sexual assault and rape by her own cousin, the Welsh prince Owain mab Urien. The enraged king had his daughter tied to a chariot and hurled from a cliff off Traprain Law, a 220-mile-high hill. God's protective hand, however, guided the chariot to a miraculously soft landing.

Aghast and dismayed, the people believed her to be a witch. She was then set adrift without any oars in a coracle down the river Forth. The people decided to let the gods deal with her. Indeed, the one true God brought her safely to Culross. There she washed ashore in the small, round boat and was discovered by Saint Serf.

Serf was now in Scotland ministering to the Picts, after serving as pope for seven years. He took in the young maid heavy with child, giving her food and shelter. A short while later, she gave birth to a boy whom she named Kentigern. Saint Serf nicknamed him Mungo, which means "dear one." Theneva and her son continued to live among the community of Saint Serf.

Raised by his mother and the monk, Kentigern grew up to be a saint. At twenty-five years of age, he became a missionary. Known as the apostle to the Britons, he built a church where the Glasgow Cathedral now stands.

Saint Theneva traveled with her son. She and Kentigern are credited with the founding of the town of Glasgow. Eventually, the princess married a prince from northern Wales, Dingad, son of Nudd. She bore five more sons and lived a happily married life. Yet her holiness was born from the strength, trust, and perseverance it took to bring her firstborn into the world.

DEALING WITH CRISIS PREGNANCIES

If Saint Theneva had not given birth to Saint Kentigern, European history would have turned out differently. Because of this apostle, the Britons became Christians. Theneva's story reminds us mothers that every child has a purpose.

Every pregnancy is conceived by God, and every child is wanted by him. Did God will the rape or sinful act that resulted in Theneva's pregnancy? No! But he allowed the child to be conceived and placed within him an immortal soul. The baby is God's way of bringing something good from something bad — even if at the time, it may not feel that way.

For some, the news of a pregnancy is a joyous occasion; for others, though, it is a scary time. The thought of having a baby can be overwhelming. This is especially true when a child is conceived in traumatic and violent circumstances. Yet, regardless of the circumstances surrounding their conception, all children come into this world for a reason. God has a mission for each one of us. All of us are destined for the everlasting happiness of heaven.

So if you are one of those mothers whose life has been turned topsy-turvy with the news that you are expecting a baby, take a deep breath and trust God. He will provide you with all that you and your child require. If need be, seek help from a local pregnancy crisis center. There, you will find material and emotional support, a little bit of wisdom, and a lot of love. You have the grace to bring to completion the good that God has begun in you (see Phil 1:6).

Those of us who have never had to face a crisis pregnancy need not waste time judging or wondering about the circumstances that led someone else to that situation. All moms need support and encouragement, especially the most vulnerable among us. Support your local pregnancy center by volunteering or donating. Pray for the women and children they serve. Beg God to give these expectant mothers the strength and courage needed to get through pregnancy, have a healthy childbirth, and make the best decisions for their little one after birth.

May all of us mommies have the faith, hope, and love we need to attain the everlasting joy God has in mind for each of us and our families.

OUR PRAYER

Father, we praise you for the gift of life. What a precious gift it is! Increase in us a love for the unborn and a devotion to their mothers. Through the intercession of Saint Theneva, may women who are experiencing crisis pregnancies, especially those who conceived through sexual assault, find the grace within themselves and the support from their communities to give their child the gift of life. We ask this through your Holy Spirit, the giver all life. Amen.

Saint Ludmila

FAST FACTS
c. 860–September 15, 921

Feast day: September 16

Patron saint of Bohemia, converts, duchesses,
and against troubles with in-laws

Children: Two — Spitignev and Vratislav

63

Ihave worked more than twenty-five years for the Catholic Church, and I have seen many grandparents taking their grandchildren to religious education classes and Mass every weekend. The reasons for this vary. Sometimes, their children are lapsed Catholics; others have children who work on Sundays; and some grandparents are raising their grandchildren. All I can say is God bless these grandparents. They have a powerful friend and example in Saint Ludmila.

Duchess Ludmila and her husband, Borivoj I, Duke of Bohemia, were converted to Christianity by the famous apostle to the Slavs, Saint Methodius, just one year into their marriage. They were the first Czech rulers to come to the Faith. The enthusiasm of the two new converts, however, failed to win over their pagan subjects. They faced so much opposition that they were exiled from their own country. In their absence, chaos ensued. Not long after their departure, they were asked to return, and peace was restored.

The duke and duchess were wise and just rulers. Together, Ludmila and Borivoj built the first church in Bohemia, Saint Clement Church. When Borivoj died, the dukedom was given to the elder of their two sons, Spitignev. After two short years, however, he passed away, and his younger brother, Vratislav, succeeded him.

Ludmila retired to a castle in Tetin after her husband's death. When it became clear to her that her son and daughter-in-law had no intention of raising their sons as Christians, she asked that the eldest boy, Wenceslaus, be allowed to live with her. Ludmila tutored and raised her grandson. Thus, the grandmother was able to ensure that the boy learned and lived the Faith.

When Wenceslaus was a young teen, his father died. Because the boy was so young, his mother, Drahomíra, ruled as regent in his place. She had the youth removed from his grandmother's home and returned to the palace. Still, Drahomíra resented the influence that Ludmila had over her son. As a Christian, Wenceslaus was a threat to her anti-Christian rule.

Drahomíra hired two noblemen to murder the elderly lady. The assassins forced their way into the castle at Tetin, found the Duchess in her bedroom, and strangled her with her own veil. When Wenceslaus was old enough to ascend to the throne, he had his grandmother's body brought to Saint George's church in Prague, where he venerated his holy grandmother, Ludmila. Many considered her a martyr for the Faith.

By her life and death, Ludmila won the graces for her grandson to follow in her footsteps. Not only did he live a Christian life, but eventually, Wenceslaus would also be martyred — by his own brother, Boleslaus. Both grandmother and grandson are saints.

THE GIFT OF FAITH

When I was young, my father would always write a note in my birthday card: "Remember, the greatest gift your mother and I ever gave you is the gift of Faith." How true! The bicycle, skateboard, Mystery Date game, and every other toy my parents gave me are long gone. My faith, however, is not only still with me but has grown with me.

Faith is indeed a gift. Like all gifts, it must be opened and used. We pass on the gift of faith to our children, but they must open it and use it, too. As heartbreaking as it is, our children do not always appreciate this great gift. They also have another gift from God called free will. As such, their rejection of the Faith is not always a reflection on their parents.

If your grown children are rejecting the Faith you've tried to share with them, be bold like Saint Ludmila. Volunteer to take your grandchildren to religious education classes and Mass on Sundays. Make it a special time for the child — get donuts afterwards or prepare and eat breakfast together. If your grandchildren live too far away to see them every week, ask if they can come visit in the summer and stay for a while. Then, you can expose them to Christian living through your words and example.

Saint Ludmilla did just that, and her grandson took her teaching and example to heart. As king, Wenceslaus was known as a kind and gracious ruler. His charity has been immortalized in the beloved Christmas carol named in his honor. Not only did he die for the Faith, but more importantly, like his saintly grandmother, he lived it. Your grandchildren will never be kings and may not become martyrs. Still, you can teach them to know, love, and serve God so that they can become saints, too.

By the way, never give up on your children. If you have cried the tears of Saint Monica, be assured that God will answer your prayers as he did hers. In the meantime, draw comfort and strength from Saint Ludmila's example and continue to hand on the Faith.

OUR PRAYER

Father in heaven, what a beautiful thing it is to see the Faith handed down generation after generation! Thank you for the gift of faith. We beg you, let the Catholic Faith be passed down generation after generation in our families. Through the intercession of Saint Ludmila, give us the wisdom, courage, and zeal to teach and live what Jesus taught and lived. We ask this in his name. Amen.

St. Elizabeth of Hungary

FAST FACTS
February 7, 1207–November 17, 1231

Feast day: November 17

Patron saint of bakers, beggars, and
Third Order Franciscans

Children: Three — Hermann II, Sophia, and Gertrude

I met my husband when I was twenty-five, which felt old at the time. Perhaps you met your husband at a later age. Or perhaps you knew your husband long before getting married. Maybe you were high school sweethearts or childhood friends. Still, I don't know anyone who has known their husband since the age of four!

Princess Elizabeth of Hungary was promised in marriage to Hermann of Thuringia at the tender age of four. She even went to live at his castle in Germany to learn the customs, language, and culture. Hermann, however, died when Elizabeth was just nine years old. She was then betrothed to the next son and now heir to the throne, Ludwig. She and Ludwig had become dear friends during her time in the court of Thuringia. Thus, when they were married in 1221, the same year Ludwig ascended the throne, the couple had a strong foundation on which to build their marriage.

In the spring of 1226, Thuringia was devastated by flood, pestilence, and famine. Ludwig was away in Italy on business for Emperor Frederick II, so Elizabeth took charge. She liberally distributed food from the castle's pantry, regal robes from her wardrobe, and ornaments from the castle to those in most need. Below the castle, which sat high on a hill, she had a hospital built. She herself often visited and nursed the patients in its twenty-eight beds. Upon his return, Ludwig was proud of the good and merciful work of his wife.

However, a family member complained to Ludwig of his wife's generous spirit. He is reported to have answered the complaints, saying, "So long as she doesn't give away the castle, I am happy with her." The ruler protected his wife's acts of charity, penance, and vigils. He was known to hold her hand as she prayed at their bedside at night. The brave Christian soldier recognized in his young wife a true warrior of God.

When Elizabeth was pregnant with their third child, Ludwig was sent to join the Sixth Crusade. Before reaching the Holy Land, he died of a fever. It took over a month for the word to get back to Elizabeth, who had just given birth to their daughter, Gertrude. She was devastated: "I have given my whole self to God and now I must also give you." The twenty-year-old widow declared, "The world with all its joys is now dead to me." She vowed never to marry again.

In time, Elizabeth found the strength to continue her work among the poor. When her brother-in-law, who was ruling as regent for her five-year-old son, did not give Elizabeth the liberty to perform her acts of charity and penance, she moved out of the castle. She went to the Franciscan convent that she had helped to build, where she sang the *Te Deum*, praising God even in her sorrow. Elizabeth did not blame God or question his goodness. On the contrary, she still had the heart to serve her true Lord and Master.

The following year, on Good Friday, Elizabeth received the dress of the Third Order of Saint Francis. While she promised chastity and obedience, her spiritual director did not allow her to make a vow of poverty. Though she desired it, her position prevented her from committing to complete and voluntary poverty. Her director knew she could do more good with her riches than she could in poverty.

So she built another hospital in Marburg. There, she devoted herself to the care of the ailing poor. She did not shy away from even the most repugnant tasks. She saw Christ in the sick: Their wounds were his wounds. She was happy to be able to tend to them.

While tending steadfastly to the ill, her own health began to decline. Elizabeth died at the tender age of twenty-four. Truly, this princess spent her life for God.

After her death, Elizabeth was buried in the church in the Marburg hospital which she had built. Immediately, miracles, especially of healing, began being reported. Examination of these miracles and of her life, plus the testimony of her confessor, handmaidens, and companions, led to her canonization less than four years after her death. Stories passed down about Elizabeth of Hungary also tell of miracles that happened while she was still alive.

One story tells of Elizabeth taking bread from the palace to distribute to the poor. While on the road to the village, she was intercepted by her husband who was on a hunting party. In order to allay the concerns of the gentry that Elizabeth was stealing from the castle, he asked to see what was in the basket she was carrying. When she removed the cloth from atop the basket, red and white roses could be seen. Ludwig was thus reassured that her acts of charity were the work of the Lord.

On another occasion, Elizabeth nursed a poor leper in her and Ludwig's own bedroom. Even for the pious Ludwig, this seemed to be going a bit too far. One account even says he was indignant, as one could imagine, at having a man with a contagious disease in his bed. Yet upon entering his own bedroom and pulling back the sheets, Ludwig saw not a leper, but the figure of Christ crucified. Indeed, Elizabeth was serving Christ in the poor and suffering.

There is no way of knowing for sure if these stories are true, exaggerated, or pure legend. I guess the extent to which you believe in miracles is the extent to which you will believe in these stories. Either way, the miracles are not what made Elizabeth a saint; rather, her cooperation with God's grace in feeding the poor and caring for the sick is.

Pope Benedict XVI, in reflecting on the life of St. Elizabeth of Hungary during one of his Wednesday general audiences, called her marriage "a clear witness to how faith and love of God and neighbor strengthen family life and deepen the matrimonial union." Her husband loved her dearly and admired her acts of charity and piety. By living her faith, she lifted him up. In fact, in Germany he is called Saint Ludwig, though he was never officially canonized by the Church as his wife was.

SANCTIFICATION THROUGH MARRIAGE

St. Elizabeth of Hungary won the respect and admiration of her husband through her virtues, especially charity. Her marriage was one of mutual love and respect, which is essential to every marriage. How do we foster this kind of mutual love and respect in our own marriages?

First, be mindful of the wonderful things your spouse does. Notice the many ways your husband reflects the love of Jesus and the providence of the Father. The more you look for virtues in him, the easier it will become to see them. Take time to write his virtues down in a notebook or journal. Then, during those times when his good qualities seem more — well — hidden, read over your lists and be reminded how virtuous your husband really is.

Next, acknowledge those good qualities and virtues to your husband and others. Compliment him and thank him. Talk nicely about him to your family and friends. On occasion, let him hear you say it. Kind words go a long way in building up, not just our children, but our husbands as well.

Practice virtues yourself — charity, patience, humility, temperance, kindness, and the like. Some virtues come naturally to us. Others we must really work to achieve. Choose one to conscientiously work on.

Finally, think of little ways to show your love for your spouse. Place a note in his lunch, leave the laundry for another day to make time to sit and snuggle with him, or make his favorite dessert for no special reason.

Our charity will overflow from our husbands to our children and out into the world around us. Indeed, we ought to use our time and talents, like St. Elizabeth of Hungary did, to serve those in need within our church and community, too. True, it gets exhausting reaching out and doing for others all the time. Jesus reminds us, though, that "what is impossible for human beings is possible for God" (Lk 18:27). We cannot be virtuous on our own. We need God's good grace. Ask him for it.

OUR PRAYER

Heavenly Father, we are in awe of all the goodness in this world you have created. We also see the hurt and suffering. May we use the virtues that we have been blessed with and those on which we are still working to help alleviate the pain and sadness of those around us. Through the intercession of St. Elizabeth of Hungary, may we have the energy to serve the needs of others, especially our husbands and children and all those with whom we come in contact. We ask this through Jesus Christ, who came to serve, not be served. Amen.

St. Margaret of Cortona

FAST FACTS
1247–February 22, 1297

Feast day: February 22

Patron saint of homeless people, single moms

Children: One son

Have you ever gone through the "Looking for Love in All the Wrong Places" phase of life? Every human being craves love; we were created for it. Sometimes, though, we get mixed up. We mistake attention or passion for love. If this has ever happened to you, you are in good company; many of the saints also had to learn to refocus their hearts. We know of St. Mary Magdalene and Saint Augustine, but St. Margaret of Cortona is another wonderful example. You see, passionate people can be great sinners, but they also make powerful saints.

St. Margaret of Cortona was a single mom. Her son was born out of wedlock, and she never married the father; she couldn't. She was the daughter of working people, while he came from nobility. Convention of the time frowned upon the mingling of the upper class with the lower class. A man of noble standing would not (publicly) associate with a woman of ill repute. And Margaret's reputation rivaled her beauty.

Margaret had been beautiful even as a young girl. She was also an only child and very much spoiled. The strong-willed girl had to be reined in often by her mother. When her mother died, Margaret lost the only influence that held her in check. Her father remarried, and Margaret was in continual and open conflict with her stepmother. She was restless and went about town trying to find ways to quell her desire for love and adventure, which men were all too eager to give her. Margaret, liking the attention, often pitted one man against another. By the age of seventeen, the young lady had quite the reputation around town. Finally, the man who had loved her most in this world, her father, kicked her out of his home. She had shamed him.

Now, Margaret had to look for work. Plus, she needed a place to stay. That is how she came to be a servant in the employment of the Italian noble Arsenio del Monte. Her beauty caught his attention, and Margaret was attracted to him, too. Eventually, they fell in love — at least, in their limited understanding of love.

As often happens when there is intimacy, Margaret got pregnant. Arsenio promised to marry her but never did. Yet he kept her well in his castle. She had nice clothes, jewels, and his attention — well, sometimes. Other times, that old feeling of loneliness crept over Margaret, even in this beautiful home. Its huge size only made the loneliness loom larger.

Having a child settled Margaret's wild spirit. She loved her son. Being a mom made her think more often of her own mother. She remembered the prayers she had taught her and recalled Bible stories her mother had told her. For the first time, Margaret was becoming conscious of her sin. Perhaps her mother's prayers from heaven were beginning to affect her heart and redirect it to the source of all love.

For nine years, Margaret lived as Arsenio's mistress in his home. Though she was always free to come and go, she was beginning to feel more and more trapped. She had, excuse the expression, made her bed and now must lie in it. So she endured the misery and deception that accompanied the lifestyle she had chosen, until one fateful day.

Arsenio's favorite hound dog came whining into her room and tugged at the hem of her dress. Fearing something was wrong, she followed it into the woods near the castle. There, the dog led her to her lover's dead body, partly decomposed and already covered with maggots. It was an awful sight. Then, her thoughts turned to his soul. She worried about the condition of his soul. Moreover, she feared the part she had played in his life of sin.

Like the prodigal son, she returned to her father's house to beg for forgiveness. Bestowing his mercy upon her, her father allowed Margaret and her son back into his home. Margaret decided that she also needed to publicly confess her sins and do penance, since this was the town in which she had gained her reputation. The shame and embarrassment this caused her father was once again too much, and, at the insistence of her stepmother, Margaret was again turned out of her family home.

With child in hand, Margaret walked to the town of Cortona, where the Franciscans had recently built a monastery. The friars placed her in the home of a modest widow and her daughter-in-law. There, Margaret began in earnest a life of reparation. She desired to outnumber her many serious sins with acts of love. She worked for her food as a midwife and nurse, always giving half of what she received to the poor. She did not charge for her services but accepted what was given to her. Seeking out the poor and suffering, her hope was to love Jesus in the least of his brethren.

What about her son in all of this? He was a blessing to her, a sign of God's love even when she was steeped in sin. Her eventual conversion had begun soon after his birth. Margaret supported her son while working. In time, he was taken in by the Franciscans to be educated. Eventually, he became a friar and priest. This made Margaret's heart very happy. After three years' probation, Margaret herself was received into the Third Order of Saint Francis.

The friars called her "the Franciscan Mary Magdalene." Her passion was for the Lord; however, at times old cravings still came upon her. She fought them with acts of penance and prayer. An intense human being, she worried whether she was loving God enough. In his mercy, Jesus would appear to her in visions to assure her of his appreciation for her love. Shortly before her death, Jesus appeared once more to Saint Margaret — this time with St. Mary Magdalene. Smiling at Margaret, Jesus told Mary Magdalene, "This is my beloved daughter." St. Margaret of Cortona died in the peace of knowing she was loved by Love himself.

SUPPORTING EACH OTHER

Single moms are my heroes. The emotional strength to raise kids on their own is a grace that can only come from God. Single moms rely on and accept that grace every day. Along with their strength, I admire their stamina, because motherhood is exhausting. There are days when I cannot wait for my husband to come home. Single moms, be they widowed, divorced, or unmarried, are strong, resilient women.

All of us mothers need help sometimes. We all feel lonely at times. It's important for moms to reach out to one another, offering play dates for the kids, going to lunch (preferably without the kids), and setting aside times to simply call to talk. Encouragement from other moms can help alleviate frustrations that accompany motherhood. We must build one another up.

Being a mom will stretch us and test us. There will be plenty of opportunities to grow in virtue (especially patience). Children give joy and meaning to life, but that does not mean raising them is always fun and easy. The vocation of motherhood is humbling in so many ways. We all mess up sometimes. Not only are we there for each other, but God is there for us, too. Through the Sacrament of Reconciliation, he gives us the grace we need to be good and holy mothers. Motherhood has a way of bringing about conversion, as it did in a big way for Saint Margaret. Motherhood changes every woman who experiences it.

OUR PRAYER

Heavenly Father, you are a God of second chances … and third, fourth, and beyond. Thank you for your mercy and forgiveness. Instill in our hearts true contrition for our sins, Lord. Through the intercession of St. Margaret of Cortona, may our hearts be always directed toward you, our one true love. We ask this in Jesus Christ, who poured out his love for us on the cross. Amen.

St. Frances of Rome

FAST FACTS
1384–March 9, 1440

Feast day: March 9

Patron saint of automobile drivers, Benedictine oblates

Children: Three — Battista, Giovanni
Evangelista, and Agnes

"**A**re you crying because you want to do God's will or because you want God to do your will?" This question was put to St. Frances of Rome by her confessor. Boy, can I relate to her tears! Likewise, I am convicted by the priest's question. If I am honest with myself, I can have a little tantrum when God does not give me what I want. Frances did, too.

Frances wanted so much to be a nun; however, her parents had already promised her in marriage to the noble Lorenzo Ponziani. No amount of tears could persuade her father otherwise. Thus, the young girl went to her confessor, hoping to find an advocate. The priest reiterated that God's will for her was marriage.

So Frances submitted to God's will. She and Lorenzo were married and, in time, had three beautiful children — two sons, Battista and Giovanni Evangelista, and a daughter, Agnes. Lorenzo treasured his wife; likewise, Frances grew to deeply love her husband. Theirs was a happy marriage that lasted forty years. Being happily married, however, does not mean that every day was a happy one.

From the beginning, Frances was thrust into high society. For her, fasting and penance were easier than feasting and entertaining. Yet her mother-in-law expected her to dress in fancy clothes, throw parties, make social visits, and join the mundane conversations of the women of high social standing. This was torture for Frances, and it took a toll on her health. For months, the newlywed wife lay sick in bed. Lorenzo was very worried about his bride, as she did not talk or eat. Then, Saint Alexis* appeared to Frances and encouraged her to trust in God's will, promising that if she did so, she would recover. Maybe Frances considered death better than life, for at first she had no response

---

* Saint Alexis was an early Roman saint whose parents arranged a marriage for him to a rich noblewoman. He desired to live poverty in imitation of Jesus, so he left home to live as a beggar. After seventeen years, he returned home, but his parents did not recognize him. Thinking he was a poor beggar, they allowed him shelter under their stairs, where he lived for the remainder of his life.

for Saint Alexis. Eventually, she simply whispered, "God's will is mine." Saint Alexis left her with the words, "Then you will live to glorify his Name." Frances regained her strength immediately and completely. Lorenzo, on hearing her story, became completely devoted to Frances and a bit in awe of her, too.

At first, Saint Frances was miserable trying to live her Christian vocation in worldly surroundings. Then, God blessed her with a friend, her sister-in-law, Vannozza, who shared her same desire to serve God in this world. Together, they attended daily Mass, served the needs of the poor and sick in their community, and helped each other balance fasting and feasting. They learned to make and receive visits joyfully, dress the part, and keep conversations godly. From Vannozza, Frances learned that by joyfully accepting her position in life, she was fulfilling God's will. Frances was grateful for Vannozza's friendship, especially since her husband was not home very much.

Lorenzo was a commander of papal troops and was often away at war. (During this time in history, the pope was just as much a political leader as he was a religious one.) Once, when Lorenzo was away, flood and disease devastated the city. Frances gave away stores from the family's granary and wine from their cellar. She sold jewels and clothes to get money for those in need. When her father-in-law discovered what she was doing, he was angry. Taking her key to the granary away, he went to see what damage had been done through her generosity. How much did she give away? To his surprise, the granary was full. But when he went to the wine cellar, not a drop of wine came out of his favorite cask. Frances took his goblet, said a quiet prayer, then turned the spigot. Wine flowed forth, filling his cup. From then on, Frances had complete control over the household and its goods.

War continued to plague Rome, as a civil war between pope and antipope broke out. Again, with Lorenzo off fighting, Frances was left in charge of the castle. Word came to the palace that her brother-in-law was taken captive. In exchange for his life, the captors wanted Lorenzo's firstborn son, Battista. Frances was trying to sneak her son out of town when she ran into her spiritual advisor. When she explained the situation, the priest told her to trust God, just as Abraham had. Frances turned around and handed her son over to the cruel governor. Then she ran to the nearest church to pray — and cry. Not long after her tear-filled supplications began to flood heaven, she felt the little arms of her son embrace her in a hug around her neck. He smiled as he told her how every horse they put him on refused to move, even the governor's, so they sent him back. He knew he would find her in the church. Her prayers were answered because she trusted.

Battista was not to remain with her for long, though. Soon, the castle was pillaged and ransacked, servants killed, and Battista taken. In divine irony, his kidnapping probably saved Battista's life, for the plague had broken out in Rome. Frances turned what was left of her home into a hospital and tried her best to care for the sick. Her son Giovanni Evangelista, who was just nine years old, died from the plague. A year later, her daughter, Agnes, also died. Frances clung even more tightly to God, as all those who were most dear to her now were gone.

Finally, the war came to an end, and a time of peace reigned over Rome. Lorenzo and Battista both returned home. Battista was a fine young man, but Lorenzo was broken, old beyond his years. For the next seven years, Frances nursed and tended to him. She also continued, with his blessings, to care for the sick and poor of the city.

The job was too big for Frances alone. With Lorenzo's support and respect, she started a lay order of women under the patronage of Saint Benedict. Frances bought the consecrated women a home where they could live in community. She herself, though, remained at the castle with Lorenzo until the day he died. His last words to her were, "I feel as if my whole life had been one beautiful dream of purest happiness. God has given me so much in your love."

Frances's ultimate vocation was one of love. This is the vocation we all have. Yet God also finally let her first dream come true. After Lorenzo died, Frances joined her Benedictine sisters. For the last four years of her life, God gave her the life she had asked for when she was only eleven. God did not tell Frances no; he was asking her to wait. He had so much more to give to her first.

THE NECESSITY OF FRIENDSHIP

We all need a friend like Vannozza — someone who will encourage us in our vocation. Having at least one mommy friend helps us survive motherhood. She is someone who listens to our troubles, big and small. We share tricks of the trade that work and give warning about those things that do not. Saint Frances found in Vannozza a friend who was experiencing the same feelings as she was. Having friends that share the same vocation lets you know you are not alone in your struggles.

Our friends influence and shape us, so we need to choose them carefully. Vannozza had the same ideals as Frances. Our friends should, likewise, have our same values, whether that friend is a sister-in-law, coworker, childhood friend, or someone you have met at a mom's group. She will help you figure out what is really important in life and to prioritize those things. We all need a little reality check now and again. A good friend is just the person to straighten us out, if need be.

A true friend will aid us in our spiritual growth. She will pray with and for us. How nice it is to have someone with whom we can discuss spiritual matters and insights, as Frances and Vannozza would do. A spiritual friend will hold us accountable in the things of God, like getting to Mass, abstaining from meat on Fridays during Lent, and other religious practices. Our desire is for one another to become saints.

In good times and bad, friends always support each other. Together, we can make a difference in our world. Like Frances and Vannozza who served the poor and sick together, friends can come together to meet a need within our communities. With a friend at our side, reaching goals becomes easier. Truly, Catholic mothers can change the world.

"Faithful friends are a sturdy shelter; / whoever finds one finds a treasure. / Faithful friends are beyond price, / no amount can balance their worth. / Faithful friends are life-saving medicine; / those who fear God will find them" (Sir 6:14–16). Though such friends are hard to find, God promises we will discover them. We ought to ask God to bless us with such godly friends. Surely, this is a prayer he will grant. If you already have a friend like that, well then, thank God.

OUR PRAYER

Heavenly Father, how good you are. You know we are too weak to make this journey alone. In your goodness, you have given us so much help. Thank you for spiritual friends — the ones on earth and the ones in heaven, like our patron saints and guardian angels. Through the intercession of St. Frances of Rome, may we always seek to do your will and await your perfect timing in answering our prayers. We ask this through our Best Friend, Jesus Christ. Amen.

St. Rita of Cascia

FAST FACTS
1381–May 22, 1457

Feast day: May 22

Patron saint of hopeless cases

Children: Two — Giovanni Antonio and Paulo Maria

Have you ever made plans that seemed to be going horribly wrong, only to have it all turn out just fine? Well, that pretty much sums up the life of St. Rita of Cascia.

Rita — Margherita Lotti — was born to Antonio and Amata Lotti in their old age. They loved their "little pearl" for the gift from God that she was. Wanting to make sure Rita was safe and provided for before their deaths, her parents arranged her marriage to a prominent man in town, Paolo Mancini. At the tender age of twelve, Rita was married. Rita understood her parents' loving intentions, even though her dream had been to become a nun.

Though Paolo, as the town watchman, had a good public reputation, as a husband, he was cruel and unfaithful. Rita bore the ill treatment with prayer and patience, trusting God to change her husband's heart.

In Italy at the time, violent feuds among rivaling families were all too common. Remember the Capulets and the Montagues of *Romeo and Juliet*? The Mancini family was involved in just such animosity with the Chiqui family. Because of this rivalry and his quick temper, Paolo had many enemies in Cascia.

Eventually, Rita's prayers and peaceful nature began to have a positive effect on her husband. His abusive manner softened toward his wife and their two sons, and he became more congenial to all. Upset with the change in Paolo's disposition, allies within his own family betrayed him. While fulfilling his duties as watchman, Paolo was ambushed and violently stabbed to death by Guido Chiqui. Despite this tragedy, Rita experienced peace amid her sorrow, knowing that her husband died in the state of grace.

At his funeral, Rita publicly forgave her husband's murderer and those responsible for his death. Nonetheless, the feud continued. Paolo's brother, Bernardo, began pressuring his nephews to avenge their father's murder. Vendetta, he explained, was necessary to defend the family's honor. Rita, on the other hand, pointed to Christ on the cross and told her sons that if Christ crucified could forgive his killers, then they should forgive their father's killers as well.

When Bernardo's persuasion seemed to be holding more sway than her own, Rita prayed and begged God not to let her sons commit any mortal sin. Within the year, both of her sons died. She accepted their deaths as an answer to her prayer and thanked God for saving their souls.

Widowed and childless, Rita thought that perhaps now she would be able to enter the convent as she had desired when she was a child. She applied for entrance to the Augustinian monastery of St. Mary Magdalene. Despite her virtuous reputation, however, Rita's request was denied. There were sisters in the monastery who were of the Chiqui family, and the superior feared the family rivalry would disturb the peace within the convent walls.

Undeterred, Rita prayed to her personal patrons, Saint Augustine, St. John the Baptist, and St. Nicholas of Tolentino, asking them to show her the way. She then reached out to her husband's family and the Chiqui family, imploring them to make peace with one another, as God would have them do. Eventually, the two families acquiesced.

Finally, six years after her husband's death, at the age of thirty-six, Rita gained admittance to the convent of St. Mary Magdalene in Cascia, where she would live the rest of her life according to the Rule of Saint Augustine. This is what she had hoped for from the beginning.

On Good Friday 1442, Rita became totally enrapt in prayer before Christ crucified on the cross. Overcome with sorrow at the pain Jesus experienced, she wanted, in some way, to relieve Jesus of his pain. No sooner had she spoken this desire to Jesus when a thorn from the crucifix fell off the crown and pierced her own head. For the last fifteen years of her life, the external stigmata caused her constant pain. Rita bore this suffering with patience and joyfulness, just as she had always borne her sufferings throughout her life.

Saint Rita's plan for her life seemed like it was all going horribly wrong, but God brought good out of it. First, through her prayers and sufferings, God saved the souls of three men — her husband and two sons. In addition, because she was a true peacemaker, Rita was able to bring reconciliation between two warring families. In the end, God blessed her with the religious vocation which she had always wanted.

PRAYING FOR OUR FAMILIES

How much do we pray for our family's salvation?

When a child or spouse is sick, we get on our knees and pray fervently for a return to health. We ask God to help them make wise decisions when faced with dilemmas and to give them success and happiness in this life. We may even pray for the future spouses of our children, as we should. In the face of job loss or potential promotion for our husbands or even ourselves, we storm heaven. In financial difficulty, we beg God to provide for us. All of this is well and good. But do we pray with as much fervor and consistency for the salvation of our families? More than anything in the world, do we want our families to make it to heaven? Even if the answer is yes, do we pray consciously and consistently for this intention?

Like Saint Rita, we ought to beseech Our Lord to protect our spouse and children from ever falling into mortal sin and to guide them to their true home in heaven. In all things, we must ask that God's will be done, for it is his will that brings about our salvation.

OUR PRAYER

Heavenly Father, thank you for the hope of eternal life which your Son gained for us. Above all things, may we desire the salvation of our families, "For here we have no lasting city, but we seek the one that is to come" (Heb 13:14). There, in heaven, with Saint Rita and all the saints, we will glorify you forever. We ask this through Christ Our Lord and Savior. Amen.

St. Margaret Clitherow

FAST FACTS
1555–March 25, 1586

Feast day: October 25

Patron saint of businesswomen

Children: Three — Henry, Anne, and William

Sometimes life just gets way too hectic. Balancing our obligations as wife, mother, employee, and volunteer makes us so dizzy, we do not know whether we are coming in the door or going out. How can we do it all?

Meet Margaret Clitherow, patron saint of businesswomen and holy wife and mom.

When Margaret married widowed John Clitherow, she helped the successful and respected butcher in his shop. Charming and witty, the young wife endeared herself to the patrons. Moreover, they appreciated her sense of fairness and generosity. Fixing fair prices, she never gouged any customer. It was known that she gave liberally to the poor. In all of this, Margaret herself proved to be a good businesswoman.

Not only did she help run a successful business, Margaret ran a loving home as well. The couple eventually had three children: Henry, Anne, and William. They were a happy family. Margaret was a wonderful wife and mother who was greatly loved. Her husband John's only qualm with Margaret was that she would not attend church — at least, not the Church of England.

You see, Margaret lived under Queen Elizabeth I and her reign of terror upon the Catholic Church. Even though her parents had converted to the new Church of England when she was just a little girl, Margaret reconverted to Catholicism three years into her marriage. The charitable acts of the Church and the faithfulness of its members despite the growing persecution drew her back into the fold.

Bold Margaret was not intimidated by the mounting tyranny against Catholics. In 1581, Catholic religious ceremonies were outlawed, and sheltering a priest was punishable by death. By 1585, it was high treason to be a Catholic priest in England. Because Margaret invited priests to say Mass in her home and hid the sacred vessels and even the priests themselves there, the Clitherow family found itself caught up in the persecutions.

In the beginning, John would pay the fines for his wife's recusancy, the penalty for her refusing to attend the services of the Church of England. As time went on and hatred for Catholics reached a fever pitch, however, even her husband could not keep her out of jail. Three times she was imprisoned; the third time, she was held for almost twenty months. Never one to waste time, she took advantage of the solitude to continue to study her faith, read the Church Fathers, and learn to read and write Latin. She even gave birth to her third child, William, in prison.

Margaret was always suspected of harboring Catholic priests and hosting Mass in her home — as indeed she was. In her home there was a "priest hole," a secret room for hiding priests, sacred vessels, and vestments. As raids on her home began, she rented another home in the city in order to keep her priest-friends safe. Though it was part of her husband's responsibility as a wealthy civic leader to report Catholic worshipers, he secretly supported his wife.

On a couple of occasions, in the secret of night, Margaret visited the gallows of Tyburn from which some of her priest-friends hung. Underneath the scaffold there, she prayed for the grace to die as a martyr. She began to desire martyrdom above all else. It was a prayer that God would soon answer.

Though her Protestant neighbors would often warn Margaret of oncoming raids, she was not home the day authorities searched and discovered the priest hole in her home. Her children and their Catholic tutor were at home, and they were taken into custody. Margaret immediately turned herself in to the authorities.

Margaret refused to enter a plea. She stated: "I know of no offense whereof I should confess myself guilty. Having made no offense, I need no trial." By forgoing a trial, Margaret spared her husband and children the agony of having to testify against her. According to English law, anyone who refused to plea was to be declared guilty and, not hanged, but pressed to death. The judge tried to stress to her the horrific barbarity of such a death, hoping to get her to accept a trial, but Margaret remained firm in her convictions. In the end, she was condemned to death.

When she was informed of her sentence, Margaret confided in a friend: "The sheriffs have said that I am going to die this coming Friday; and I feel the weakness of my flesh which is troubled at this news, but my spirit rejoices greatly. For the love of God, pray for me and ask all good people to do likewise." Sometimes we think martyrs are superhuman. The truth is that they are very much human, but they rely on supernatural graces. Margaret would rely on God's grace to sustain her in her wish for martyrdom.

The night before her death, the future saint experienced an agony of fear. Following the example of Jesus on the night before he was to die, Margaret prayed intensely. The Father answered with an infusion of graces beyond human understanding. Thus, Margaret became calm and peaceful. She even smiled while walking barefoot to the tollbooth on the bridge where her execution would take place. The mother had sent her shoes to her daughter, Anne, who had been kept in custody until her mother's death. With her freedom, Anne received the shoes and a note from her mother encouraging her to follow in her footsteps.

On Ouse Bridge, on March 25, 1586 (Good Friday that year), Margaret was stripped and laid on the ground with a sharp rock the size of a fist under her back. Her hands were stretched out in the form of a cross and tied to two posts. Then the door to her own house was placed upon her. Slab weights were dropped one at a time upon the door until the rock broke her back. She did not cry out, but continually repeated, "Jesus, have mercy on me!" After fifteen minutes of agony, she fell silent. Her body was then left under the more than 600 pounds of stone slabs for six hours to assure her death.

The citizens of York were appalled at such a cruel execution. "You will make Papists of us all!" the angry people of the city shouted at the magistrate's house. Even the queen expressed dismay over Margaret's death. She declared that no woman should be executed in such a horrific manner. As a result, the other two women martyrs of this time, Anne Line and Margaret Ward, were hanged for their crime of harboring priests.

Margaret's daughter, Anne, did indeed follow in her mother's footsteps. In 1593, she was again briefly imprisoned for her refusal to attend Church of England services. Then, in 1598, she gave her life to Jesus, not as a martyr, but as a nun at Saint Ursula's Convent in Louvain. Henry and William studied abroad to become priests. Henry eventually returned to England as a missionary. The children bore the fruit of their mother's sacrifice.

St. Margaret Clitherow, loving mother, faithful wife, flourishing businesswomen, was the first woman to be martyred under Queen Elizabeth's religious suppression. In 1970, St. Margaret Clitherow was canonized by Pope Paul VI as one of the forty English martyrs.

FINDING TIME FOR PRAYER

Margaret homeschooled her children, took care of their home, worked outside the home in her husband's butcher shop, and was loved and respected by her family, friends, and customers. Even with a household and a business to run, Margaret found time to pray every day for one and a half hours. Perhaps that's the secret of her success in both life and death.

If we *try* to find the time to pray during our hectic day, we won't. Instead, we must *make* the time. We all know that relationships grow stronger when we communicate and share with each other. But did you know that Jesus desires this kind of relationship with you? He wants to hear about your day, your plans, your concerns. Tell him. Then sit and listen, for he has thoughts he wishes to share with you, too.

Whenever possible, try to go to Mass or adoration. Perhaps on your commute to work you can pray the Rosary, pop in a religious CD, listen to a Catholic podcast, or tune in to a Christian music station. How wonderful it would be to wake up a half hour earlier to read and meditate upon a Bible passage. If you are a mother of an early riser (aka a toddler), you may have to wait for nap time to sit with Jesus for a little while. Before bed, turn the TV off a little sooner and talk to the Lord about your day. Any of these efforts will be greatly blessed by God, and you just may find yourself more productive throughout the day. With greater peace and love in your heart, you will be able to handle any challenges your day throws at you. Your attitude will be more positive. Most of all, you will have the graces to make the many sacrifices asked of you as a mommy, a wife, and a businesswoman.

OUR PRAYER

Father, we praise you for the gift of our Catholic Faith and the priesthood. Through the intercession of St. Margaret Clitherow, inspire in us a greater love and respect for priests. Grant us a sense of awe for our own vocation. It, too, is a type of martyrdom. May the fruit of our prayer be the grace to joyfully make the sacrifices, big and small, that will be asked of us today. And Father, may we live life in such a way that all those around us may know that we are Catholic Christians, followers of your Son, Jesus Christ, in whose name we pray. Amen.

St. Jane Frances de Chantal

FAST FACTS
January 28, 1572–December 13, 1641

Feast day: August 12

Patron saint of children separated from
parents and loss of parents

Children: Six — Two died in infancy; three
daughters and one son survived

Could you forgive the person who shot and killed your husband? What if it was an accident? Does that make it easier to forgive? Could you smile and say "Hello" when you saw him out and about in town? Would you invite him over for dinner? Neither could St. Jane Frances de Chantal — at first.

Saint Jane Frances was a cheerful young lady, witty, with a lively disposition. When her father, the French parliamentary president, arranged a marriage for her to the baron of Chantal, Christophe de Rabutin, she was happy. She was infatuated with the young baron. At the age of twenty, she was married. Jane and Christophe were deeply devoted to one another.

Unfortunately, Jane entered a household that was in debt. Yet she managed her husband's estate so well that in time all debt was paid off. The household staff loved and respected her. Even while in debt, the lady of the house made sure the staff was compensated fairly. Likewise, the poor who came to their door were given alms in some form and treated with the utmost charity. No matter how busy life got, Jane went to daily Mass and requested that the staff do the same. To make it easier on them, she had Mass celebrated right there in the castle. Saint Jane Frances was the epitome of an efficient domestic engineer!

In time, the young wife became a doting mother. Sadly, the first two children she bore died in infancy. I can only imagine the excitement and worry that the couple felt when Jane realized she was pregnant again. Praise be to God! Jane Frances delivered a healthy baby girl, Marie. A son, Celse Benigne, was born soon after, followed by two more girls whose names seem to have been lost to history. Life seemed wonderful and complete, until that fateful day.

While on a hunting trip, the baron was accidentally shot by a friend. His friend who had shot him begged for forgiveness, but Christophe told him that there was nothing to forgive, as the shooting was an accident. Jane Frances, however, did not feel the same way. Christophe encouraged her to forgive his friend, but she could not find it in her broken heart to do that. After suffering for nine days, the Baron de Chantal succumbed to his injury. Following her husband's death, Jane Frances fell into a deep depression. After only seven wonderful years of marriage, she found herself widowed with four young children. She decided, at her father's suggestion, to return to her childhood home in Dijon. Not long afterward, her difficult father-in-law demanded that Jane and the children return to the family castle and continue to manage the estate. Under the threat of her children losing their inheritance, the young widow resumed her duties as the Baroness de Chantal. Though on the inside she mourned terribly, on the outside she remained cheerful in her dealings with her father-in-law and all with whom she came in contact. All the while, she prayed and asked God to heal her broken heart.

Not until she heard a Lenten homily given by Bishop Francis de Sales a couple of years later did her path to healing begin. First, as God made it known to her through that sermon, she would have to forgive her husband's friend. She took baby steps — first by greeting him on the street whenever she saw him. In time, she was able to invite him to her home, where she was finally able to voice her forgiveness. Ultimately, the Baroness de Chantal became the godmother of the man's child. God gave Jane Frances the graces she needed to do what she had to do: forgive.

Jane Frances de Chantal grew to be good friends with St. Francis de Sales. He became her spiritual advisor. Having no desire to marry again, she asked about the possibility of entering a convent. Until her children were older and provided for, he told her, that desire would have to wait. In the meantime, the baroness's works of charity continued. Anyone who came to her door received soup and bread. Sometimes the same beggar would come back over and over again for food, even in the same day. When asked why she did not send the returning beggar away, she replied, "What if God turned me away when I came back again and again with the same request?" By focusing on the needs of others and helping them, the widow was helping to heal her own heart.

Eventually, with the blessing of her father, her brother who was the archbishop of Bourges, and Francis de Sales, Jane Frances de Chantal started the Congregation of the Visitation. Her eldest daughter was married, her son was being educated by her brother and provided for by her father, and the two younger girls wanted to join their mother in religious life. Soon, they were joined by other women who, because of age, widowhood, or health, were rejected by traditional religious orders. Although cloistered, they still managed to reach out to those in need. During the Plague of 1628, the nuns converted their convent into a hospital.

Before her death, Jane Frances established eighty-six Visitation convents. Once again, she found fulfillment in her vocation. St. Jane Frances de Chantal was blessed to serve God in married life as a wife, in single life as a widow, and in religious life as a Visitation nun.

****

Try as I might, I could not find out the names of the two youngest daughters who entered the convent with their mother. Then a thought dawned on me that made me give up. When a woman enters religious life, her life is not her own anymore. This is especially true of nuns who are cloistered behind convent walls: Their lives are hidden in Christ. A religious even receives a new name, for she has received a new calling from God. Thus, I decided to let the names of the two younger daughters remain lost in Christ.

Then another thought hit me: Our lives as mothers are similar to nuns and religious sisters in that regard. When we become mothers, our lives are not our own anymore, either. Like Saint Jane Frances, we live and do for others, especially our children. To reflect the new vocation given to us by God, we also receive a name change: We are now called "Mommy." The title of "Mommy" means we are called to serve God through the children he gives us. As we learn from Saint Jane Frances's life, the well-being of our children comes before the pursuit of our own dreams. In this way, a mother dies to self and becomes more like Christ.

DEALING WITH DEPRESSION

Depression can be a very serious matter for mothers. Some experience it postpartum. The death of a child or a spouse can also trigger depression. Even the monotony of everyday life can lead to bouts of depression. Likewise, worries about family issues can cause anxiety. Sometimes there is no cause or "trigger"; depression is a physiological reality for many people.

First and foremost, know that suffering from depression or anxiety is nothing to be ashamed of. Most people feel depressed or anxious at times, especially when dealing with life's struggles or major loss, as St. Jane Frances de Chantal faced. If you or someone you know is struggling with depression, you might find it helpful to take note of some of the things St. Jane Frances de Chantal did to help herself overcome her bout with depression:

- **Tell someone:** Jane Frances told her spiritual advisor how she was feeling, and she followed his advice.
- **Do something, even if you do not feel like it**: Jane Frances concentrated on helping others and, in doing so, focused less on herself and her feelings.
- **Pray**: Jane Frances continued to pray and go to daily Mass, even though she was experiencing the dark

night of the soul and perceived no consolation from God. Yet, through her perseverance, she did receive the grace she needed to overcome her depression. Part of that healing process included forgiving her husband's friend, something she could only do by God's merciful grace.

There are times, though, when nothing seems to help. Time does not lessen the pain. At that point, it is important to seek professional help.

My family has fought the battle of depression. And yes, it affects the whole family, for, as Saint Paul points out, if one member suffers, all suffer with her (see 1 Cor 12:26). My eldest daughter has been in the trenches battling the disease. She had no triggers — no experienced loss, no family issues, nothing to point to and say, "This is why you feel so bad." On the outside, her life looked great. It was her senior year, she had straight A's throughout high school, played field hockey, performed in school plays, and was chosen as homecoming queen. Inside, however, a dark storm was brewing. Even in prayer, sinister thoughts invaded her mind. We were clueless about her struggle, and she could not find the words to tell us. What I mistook for "senioritis" and the growing pains of adolescence was actually clinical depression. We had no idea until the day came when she planned to kill herself.

I am happy to say that today, my daughter is alive and well. She told someone who, in turn, told us. We got her the help she needed, though finding just the right treatment and medication took some time. Working in the autism department at her school enabled her to focus less on herself and more on helping others. And when she couldn't pray, we prayed for her. Today, she is a recent college graduate in biology hoping to make a difference in the world so that others do not have to go through all that she did.

Clinical depression is a serious illness that needs treatment. If you or someone you know is down emotionally and cannot get up, talk to a doctor. It may require some coping skills or a few counseling sessions. Perhaps medication will be prescribed, because sometimes the chemicals in the brain stop processing properly, just like a pancreas may stop processing insulin correctly. Just as there is treatment for those with diabetes, there is treatment for those with depression. Never feel ashamed about needing help. Families need their mommies and want them to be healthy and happy.

OUR PRAYER

Heavenly Father, we praise you for the gift of forgiveness. Thank you for sending your Son so that forgiveness may be ours. Through the intercession of St. Jane Frances de Chantal, may we always be able to lavishly give and receive forgiveness. And if we ever find it difficult to ask for forgiveness or to give it, Father, may our hearts be stirred by Jesus who begged you to forgive his enemies. We ask this in his Sacred Heart. Amen.

St. Louise de Marillac

FAST FACTS
August 12, 1591–March 15, 1660

Feast day: March 15

Patron saint of social workers

Children: One — Michel

A special aspect of the vocation to motherhood is the calling to be a caretaker. While all moms are called to take care of their families, for some that calling takes on special meaning when a family member gets sick or a child with special needs comes into the family. Taking care of a spouse or child with a terminal illness draws a mother closer to the cross of Christ. While having a child with special needs may also have its crosses, it is also a beautiful blessing. St. Louise de Marillac experienced both of these realities.

Louise never knew her mother, who died when Louise was very young. Her father, Louis de Marillac, Lord of Ferrires, died when she was only twelve. So her uncle, who looked after her welfare, arranged a marriage for Louise. At the age of twenty-one, she was united to Anthony LeGras, an impressive young official in the queen's service. Louise settled into her vocation as wife and grew to truly love Anthony.

Anthony and Louise had a happy marriage. She bore him a son, whom they named Michel. As he grew, Louise realized that Michel had special needs that required extra nurturing from her. She was very devoted to her little family.

Louise was, likewise, attentive to her spiritual life. This faithful woman wrote up for herself a "Rule of Life in the World" on which she structured her day. A typical day included Mass and Holy Communion, the Little Office of the Blessed Virgin Mary, meditation, spiritual reading, penance/fasting, the Rosary, and maintaining her household. She also made time to entertain guests and perform works of charity. She did her best to preserve a balanced life.

In 1621, Anthony became ill and eventually bedridden. His chronic illness weighed heavily on her, physically and emotionally. After two years of caring for him, she became depressed. She wondered if she was, indeed, meant for married life. Perhaps God had wanted her to be a nun. She had felt a calling to religious life when she was younger. Maybe she should have tried to enter a convent. She shared her doubts with her confessor, the good St. Francis de Sales, who reassured her of her vocation as wife and mother. In prayer, Louise promised to take care of her husband for as long as God willed. She also resolved not to remarry if Anthony did not recover.

For almost three more years, she attentively took care of her husband's every need. Despite her own frail health, she endured long days, and sometimes nights, nursing him. Louise fulfilled her vows, loving and cherishing Anthony in good times and bad, in sickness and in health, until death did part them.

After the death of her husband, St. Louise de Marillac and her son had to move, a sad and difficult decision for her, but one necessitated by lack of finances. Yet God had his reasons. Because of this move, Louise met St. Vincent de Paul. The good priest recognized in this frail widow an intelligence and endurance that he needed to help with his missions for the poor. He asked Louise to lead some ladies into rural areas and dissolute parts of the city to bring aid and comfort to the sick and destitute.

What started out as five women quickly grew into a community, with Saint Louise as their spiritual mother. Even though neither she nor St. Vincent de Paul ever had any intentions of starting a new religious community, it was God's will. The Daughters of Charity, as they became known, were different than the nuns of their day. They balanced their time between prayer and apostolate. Not confined by convent walls, they went out into the dingy streets of the city and down the dusty roads of the country to care for the sick and neglected. Saint Louise and her sisters founded hospitals and orphanages throughout France.

Before her death in 1660, St. Louise de Marillac established forty convents. The Daughters of Charity would continue to grow into a worldwide order dedicated to caring for the poorest and most ill of God's children. Today, more than 350 years later, the Daughters of Charity are at the heart of many of our Catholic hospitals.

CHARITY STARTS AT HOME

The charity that St. Louise de Marillac spread throughout the world began at home. In taking care of her husband and son, Louise was being prepared by God for her life's mission. She gained the patience, tenderness, and diligence needed to do the work God had in mind for her by doing everyday tasks at home. Most important was the love that she practiced while fulfilling her responsibilities. Subsequently, when the time was right, this selfless, humble woman made her mark on the world.

The everyday responsibilities of being a wife and mom provide us with lots of opportunities to become saints. Motherhood is a daily call to die to self. Whether it is changing a stinky diaper, going to the grocery store for the umpteenth time this week, or picking up dirty socks that no one else apparently sees lying in the middle of the floor, we have many chances to show love through service.

Sometimes in the mundane, everyday chores of motherhood, we lose sight of the bigger picture. Every little act we perform for our family has meaning. When done with love, even changing diapers can be sanctifying. Fixing dinners, folding laundry, and checking homework, believe it or not, are among the most important works on earth. I am not exaggerating!

Families are the foundation of the world. The stronger our families are, the better our society will be. By serving our husbands and children, we are modeling self-sacrificing love. That's the love we take out into the world. Our children, too, go out and spread the love and respect they learn from family living. God uses us mothers to change the world, even if it is just our little part of it.

OUR PRAYER

Heavenly Father, we praise you for the many opportunities you give us to grow in holiness. Thank you for the love you lavish upon us. I beg you, Father, to teach us to be generous in giving that same love to our families and to the world around us. Through the intercession of St. Louise de Marillac, may we dedicate our lives to serving others. In Jesus' name, we pray. Amen.

St. Elizabeth Ann Seton

FAST FACTS

August 28, 1774–January 4, 1821

Feast day: January 4

Patron saint of Catholic schools, widows,
and against the death of a child

Children: Five — Anna Maria, William II,
Richard, Catherine, and Rebecca Mary

"Hazard yet forward!" Boy, are there days when I can totally relate to this motto of St. Elizabeth Ann Seton! A glance at Mother Seton's life, and you will understand why this became her battle cry.

In her forty-six years on this earth, she lost her mother, her baby sister, her father-in-law, and her own father, then her husband after six years of happy marriage, her sister-in-law who was her best friend, and two of her three daughters. Her husband lost his business and had to declare bankruptcy. When she converted to Catholicism, she lost the support of her family and many friends. With no way of providing for her five young children, she had to move from New York to Baltimore, and she considered moving to Canada before heading out to remote western Maryland to start the first girls' Catholic school, the first Catholic orphanage, and the first religious community for women in the United States. Despite all her hardships, St. Elizabeth Ann Seton went forward and became the first United States-born canonized saint.

Phew! That is a lot in a short forty-six years. Let's go back to the beginning.

When Elizabeth Ann Bayley was just three years old, her mother died, probably while giving birth to her baby sister, who died less than a year later. Her father remarried, knowing that his two surviving daughters would need a mother. The young girl quickly bonded with her stepmother, Charlotte Amelia Barclay. Active in her church and social ministry, Amelia often took Elizabeth Ann, or Betty, as she was called, along on visits to the sick and poor — a practice that Elizabeth would continue throughout the rest of her life.

Doctor Richard Bayley, Betty's father, was often absent from his family. His first love was his work in medicine, and this took a toll on his marriage. Doctor Bayley and Amelia separated when Betty was sixteen years old. After this, Amelia rejected Betty and her older sister, Mary, and they were no longer welcome in the family home. To complicate matters, Doctor Bayley decided to go overseas to study, abandoning his two daughters. Eventually, their paternal uncle took charge of the girls.

Understandably, a sense a loneliness and desolation overcame Elizabeth Ann Bayley. She turned to reading and praying with Scripture to find consolation. She also found comfort in the liturgy of the Anglican church. Betty's grandfather was the prominent pastor of Saint Andrew's church on Staten Island, which was part of the Church of England (or Anglican Church as it was called after the War for Independence). Betty found such joy in communion that she was known to go to two services on Sundays just to be able to receive twice. The closeness to Jesus that she felt in Scripture, prayer, and at church assured her that she was indeed loved, even in her feelings of abandonment.

While God was her first love, Elizabeth Ann Bayley fell deeply in love with and married William Seton. The early years of their marriage were the happiest days of her life. During their fourth year of marriage, however, William's father died. The young couple welcomed William's six younger siblings into their home, in addition to their own young children: Anna Maria, William II, and baby Richard. The loving couple would add two more daughters, Catherine and Rebecca Mary, to complete their large family. Because of his father's death, William also took charge of the family's importing business. Then, with the onset of the War of 1812, things began to fall apart.

William always suffered from tuberculosis, though it was under control. With war waging, the family business began to experience difficulties. Several ships were lost at sea. The stress on William caused his tuberculosis to flare up. As William's business failed, so did his health.

In an attempt to recover his health, Elizabeth took her husband, along with their oldest daughter, eight-year-old Anna Marie, to Italy, leaving her four other children and William's two youngest siblings with her sister-in-law and best friend, Rebecca. (William's two sisters and two brothers had been sent to boarding school.) It was their hope that a visit to the warmer climate of a family friend's home in Pisa would strengthen and revive him. When they arrived, however, the family was ordered onto a little rowboat and taken to a quarantine station. After twenty-five days confined in a room in the drafty old stone building, the Setons were allowed to leave. William, too weak to walk, had to be carried. He died two days after Christmas with his praying wife by his side in the home of family friend and business partner, Filippo Filicchi. As one who always felt deep attachment and strong emotions, Elizabeth grieved greatly. Yet she trusted what she simply called "The Will" — that is, God's will for her life, which she knew to always be for her good, even when it did not feel like it.

Elizabeth and her daughter stayed in Italy with her husband's business partner, who was Catholic. While there, Elizabeth began to experience a strong desire for the true Bread of Life. She admired the beauty of the Catholic churches that lifted her heart and mind to God. She took solace in the thought that she, who had lost her own mother at so tender an age, had a Blessed Mother in heaven. By the time she returned to her home in New York, Elizabeth was seriously and prayerfully considering entering the Catholic Church, though she knew it would cause grave disapproval in her extended family.

"I will go peacefully and firmly to the Catholic Church; for if faith is so important to our salvation, I will seek it where true faith first began, seek it among those who received it from God himself." With these words, St. Elizabeth Ann Seton took the bold step of entering the Catholic Church. She made her profession of faith in New York City's only Catholic church at the time, Saint Peter's. Immediately, she was disowned by her husband's family. Friends stopped associating with her. At the academy where she taught as a way of supporting her family, word got out about her conversion. Parents began to withdraw their students from the school. New York's anti-Catholic laws had been lifted a few years earlier, but sometimes laws change faster than hearts.

Fluent in French, she was considering moving to Catholic-friendly Québec when she met Sulpician Father Louis Dubourg, president of Saint Mary's College in Baltimore. He suggested that she open a school for girls in his city; so the widow moved south with her children. Her boys were able to attend Saint Mary's, and the girls went to school with her.

The opportunity then came for Elizabeth to travel out west to the mountains of Emmitsburg, Maryland, to establish an all-girls Catholic school. There, in the valley of what she called Mary's mountain, the educator opened Saint Joseph's Academy and Free School to provide an education for the poor girls in the area. Thus, St. Elizabeth Ann Seton was a pioneer in Catholic education in the United States.

Soon, a small group of women began sharing Mother Seton's mission of education and care for the poor, including her daughter Anna and her brother's widow, Cecilia (who became Catholic and joined her in Emmitsburg after her husband's death). On July 19, 1813, the first eighteen Sisters of Charity of Saint Joseph, including St. Elizabeth Ann Seton, professed their vows of poverty, chastity, and obedience. The order continued to grow throughout her lifetime. By the time of Mother Seton's death, the Sisters of Charity had opened schools, orphanages, and hospitals in Maryland, Pennsylvania, New York, and Ohio. Even today, orders of religious women can trace their mission to serve God's poor and afflicted to St. Elizabeth Ann Seton and her Sisters of Charity.

****

St. Elizabeth Ann Seton's love for Scripture was real. At least two of her Bibles have survived to this day. Insight into her spirituality can be gleaned from the underlining and notes on the pages. (Yes, it is well and good to write in your study Bibles! So, go ahead, mark them up — highlight, underline, jot down notes — it's OK!)

In one of her Bibles, Mother Seton underlined the phrase "Look up," in both in Genesis 15:5 and Genesis 22:13. To her, the saying gave hope.

In Genesis 15:5, God promised Abraham descendants as numerous as the stars. "*Look up* at the sky," God told Abraham, "and count the stars, if you can. Just so ... will your descendants be." God was giving Abraham hope. The cool thing about this hope God was giving to Abraham — he made the promise in broad daylight. Verse 12 begins, "As the sun was about to set ..." In other words, when God told Abraham to look up and count the stars, Abraham couldn't because it was daylight! He couldn't see the stars — yet. Still, he knew that stars too numerous to count were there. Isn't that the essence of hope? To know, even when we cannot perceive. To trust God even when we do not understand and put our faith in him.

Then, in Genesis 22, we read that Abraham's faith was tested even further. God asked Abraham to sacrifice his only beloved son, Isaac. Surely not understanding, Abraham obeyed. As you know, before the knife touched his son, an angel of the Lord stopped him. He had passed the ultimate test. Then, Abraham "*looked up* and saw a single ram" (Gn 22:13). Sometimes the answer, the hope, we are looking for is right there in front of us. I am not sure why we don't see it. Nonetheless, in God's perfect timing, he will reveal it to us. We need only to be obedient and trust.

In her trials, St. Elizabeth Ann Seton saw opportunities to trust in God. Therefore, even amid difficulties and sorrows, she experienced peace. In desolation, both physical and spiritual, she recognized purification. In all situations, she trusted that "The Will" was drawing her closer to perfection.

So, when the world around you is falling apart and things just don't seem to make sense, follow Elizabeth Ann Seton's example: Look up!

EDUCATION STARTS AT HOME

Following St. Elizabeth Ann Seton's example, we need to be reading our Bibles. We need to spend time in prayer, reflecting and meditating on Jesus' life. Getting to know Christ is essential to parenting. As Saint Jerome said, "Ignorance of Scripture is ignorance of Christ." If we do not know Jesus, how can we teach our children about him?

Our main mission as parents is to help our children know, love, and serve God. We teach them in word and action. St. Elizabeth Ann Seton understood this. She provided her daughters with their education and made sure her sons received a good Catholic education. Furthermore, her children witnessed their mother helping needy neighbors, sick family members and friends, and widows with small children. Mother Seton taught her children, and many others, not only the three "R's" of reading, 'riting, and 'rithmetic, but also the most important "R" of all: religion.

The *Catechism of the Catholic Church* tells us that "the home is the first school of Christian life" (1657). Whether we send our children to Catholic school, public school, or homeschool, as parents we are the first and most important educators of our children. We can never totally relinquish the responsibility of teaching our children to any institution. Our children will always learn at home what is important in life, what to value, and what to believe. As parents, we instill this into our children from the earliest stages of their lives. Our influence continues, even if it lessens, into their teen and young adult years. As they grow older, they will still turn to us and ask our advice. We never stop educating our children.

So, let's open our Bibles. Within its pages we will find plenty of advice and wisdom on how to raise our children. God entrusted them to us. He has also sent a "How To" manual on the important things in life through his Word. Let us learn so that we may teach.

OUR PRAYER

Heavenly Father, we look up to you and place our trust in you. Thank you for entrusting us with the children you have given us. Along with our husbands, you have called us to be the first teachers of our children. Through the intercession of St. Elizabeth Ann Seton, may we also be the best of teachers. We ask this through Jesus Christ, the best of all teachers. Amen.

Bl. Anna Maria Taigi

FAST FACTS
May 29, 1769–June 9, 1837

Feast day: June 9

Patron of housewives, victims of verbal abuse

Children: Seven — Anna, Camillo, Alessandro,
Luigi, Maria, Sophia, and Luisa

"Wives should be subordinate to their husbands as to the Lord" (Eph 5:22). In a day and age and country where independence is valued over interdependence, and feminism has been hijacked to mean we do not need men, this verse is often swept under the rug. Yet for us wives, as Bl. Anna Maria Taigi shows us, such humility and obedience are necessary to get to heaven.

Anna Maria married Domenico Taigi at a young age. She enjoyed being a wife, going shopping, keeping house, and dressing up to go out on the town with her husband. Not long after being married, though, she went to Saint Peter's Basilica in Rome where she had a conversion. While in prayer, a movement of grace helped her realize that she lived more for the world than for God. She went to confession, renounced her worldliness, and resolved to change her ways.

Anna shared her conversion story with her husband. She sought his blessing, knowing that her reformation would affect him, too. Being a pious man, Domenico assented to Anna's desire to forgo the luxuries of life, perform acts of penance, and spend more time in prayer. Anna gave up wearing fancy clothes and jewelry. Now, going to puppet shows and museums became more penance than pleasure, but she went with Domenico whenever he asked, wanting to please him. She was subject to her husband and happily accepted these penances over her own self-sacrifices.

The obligations of married life came before her desire for prayer and penance. For instance, when she was pregnant or nursing, Anna relinquished her normal fasting and ate well for the sake of her baby's nourishment. If a family member was sick, she herself tended to them, even if it meant missing Mass or her devotionals. The devout mother recognized that family life provided many opportunities to practice virtue.

Her husband was a butler for an Italian prince. After a day

spent managing the castle's many servants and seeing to the prince's constant demands, Domenico often came home in a bad mood. As soon as he walked into the house, Anna stopped whatever she was doing, be it housework or entertaining guests (even important guests like royalty or prelates) and ministered to her husband's needs. When he used bad words or spoke ill of the servants, she would not correct him at that moment, but quieted his spirit with words of affirmation about the good that he had done that day. Biographer Albert Bessieres, SJ, tells us that Domenico admitted there were times when his actions needed correction. "She could give advice charitably, and I owe it to her that I was corrected of certain faults. She corrected you with a kindliness that cannot be described, for all her ways so disarmed you that you were irresistibly obliged always to do what was pleasing to her for the good of the whole house." By overlooking her husband's faults and seeking his virtues, Anna maintained peace in her home.

Blessed Anna Maria considered marriage one of the highest missions from heaven and understood the grave responsibility of raising her children in the Faith. The mother and her four children (sadly, her other three children died in infancy) began every day with family morning prayer. When they were old enough, Anna taught them their catechism. They prayed the Rosary on their knees after supper. Anna kept her children busy — not with sports and recreational activities, as we tend to do today, but with chores and charitable works which benefited their home, church, and community. She had the wisdom to know that raising children in the Lord would have a profound social and moral impact.

On Sundays, after Mass, mother and daughters would visit the sick. One of her daughters, Sophia, recalled her mother visiting a cancer patient. When Anna would come into her presence, the woman would exclaim, "Here is my angel!" Her mother would clean and rebandage the foul-smelling wounds. Sophia herself could not stand the sight and smell of this poor patient's sores. When Sophia questioned her mother about her ability to withstand the smell, Anna had to admit it was repugnant. "But smell the fragrance of her soul; she will go straight from that bed to paradise." Blessed Anna Maria understood the role suffering has in purifying our souls and preparing us for heaven. Anna Maria was willing to suffer for the sake of poor souls. Sometimes she offered self-imposed mortifications to help a sinner see the error of his ways and repent. Other times, Jesus sent her terrible sufferings to atone for the sins of others who could not or would not make reparations themselves. These sufferings would sometimes be severe enough to confine her to bed. In October of 1836, she fell so ill that, this time, she would not recover. Bedridden, she continued patiently to offer all her suffering for poor souls. On June 9, 1837, Blessed Anna Maria died as peacefully as she lived.

✳✳✳✳✳✳✳✳✳✳

Bl. Anna Maria Taigi was a mystic. A mystic is someone who has a personal experience of God in a way that no human effort could produce; it is a truly extraordinary gift from God. Yet being a mystic is not what made Blessed Anna Maria holy. Her ardent desire for holiness and her earnest efforts to please God are the reasons Our Lord chose her to be in mystical union with him.

Blessed Anna Maria could physically hear God speak to her. After she prayed and asked for expiatory suffering to console Jesus and save sinners, God consented. Bessieres relates that God told her: "I destine you to convert sinful souls; to console priests, prelates, and even my Vicar. You will have to fight against a crowd of creatures subject to a thousand passions. You will meet many treacherous souls. You will be made a laughing stock. You will endure it for love of me. ... I shall myself guide you by the hand to the altar of sacrifice." Indeed, she suffered much, both physically and emotionally, because of her desire to help save souls. Being blessed with locutions set Anna Maria's heart on fire with a greater love for God. He, in turn, asked of her a greater part in his plan for the salvation of souls.

Blessed Anna Maria was given another extraordinary gift. A globe of light, like a mystic mini-sun, shone ever before her. In it, she could she see present happenings, foresee future events, read hearts, and hear thoughts. Before even talking to a person, she knew his or her physical and moral state. God would even reveal to her the destiny of the dying. What a grave responsibility it is to have a share in God's omnipotence! Our Lord charged Anna Maria with correcting, counseling, and encouraging people, from those she passed on the streets to powerful politicians, bishops, and even the pope himself. In obedience and humility, in word and deed, Blessed Anna Maria revealed that holiness and union with God is available to all.

We may not have the extraordinary gifts that Blessed Anna Maria had; still, God has given us each unique gifts and talents. Like Blessed Anna Maria, we are to use our gifts to help others draw closer to Our Lord. Are you called to be a catechist and instruct little ones in the Faith? If the thought of teaching terrifies you but you are compassionate, then maybe God desires you to visit the homebound and bring them Communion. Do you have leadership and organizational skills? These strengths can be used to run a fundraising event for your church. Think about what gifts and talents God has given you; then ask him how he wants you to use them.

THE POWER OF CATHOLIC MOTHERHOOD

There is a great line from the first of the Toby McGuire *Spider-man* movies: "With great power comes great responsibility." All

Catholics, through the sacraments, Sacred Scripture, and the teachings of the Church, have great power. It is the power to become saints.

Bl. Anna Maria Taigi, while she was a great mystic, achieved sanctity by striving to do God's will in living an ordinary life. We are called to do the same. As Catholics, we have all the means necessary. We need only accept and use the graces God sends us to achieve our goal.

As mothers, we have another great power — the influence we have over our families. Yes, we are called by God to be subject to our husband as head of the family, just as we are subject to Christ as head of the Church. Still, we would be foolish not to think we have tremendous sway over our husbands. Remember how Eve influenced Adam? OK, that's a bad example! Bl. Anna Maria Taigi's inspirational impact on her husband, on the other hand, is a good example. She always encouraged him to be the best man he could be and was patient with him. We should, likewise, use our power to positively impact our husbands.

Finally, as mothers, we have "power" or, more accurately, authority over our children. By virtue of the fourth commandment, our children are obliged to honor and obey us. Thus, we are above all responsible for bringing them up to know, love, and serve the Lord.

Now, we cannot make our children saints. We can, however, direct them to the way of sanctity. We cannot make our husbands holy, but we can encourage them in their virtues. One thing is for sure, as the life of Anna Maria Taigi demonstrates: We can achieve blessedness by taking advantage of the everyday opportunities of our ordinary lives to grow in virtue, holiness, and love of God.

With the great power of the sacraments, Scripture, and the teachings of the Church comes the great responsibility to become a saint!

OUR PRAYER

Heavenly Father, you are the source of grace for all marriages. Thank you for our marriages. May husbands and wives help each other become holy, as you, Father, are holy. Through the intercession of Bl. Anna Maria Taigi, grant that we may always love and respect each other. We ask this through Jesus Christ, the true master of our marriages. Amen.

Eliza Vaughan

FAST FACTS
October 8, 1810–January 24, 1853

Feast day: January 24

Patron of priestly vocations

Children: Fourteen — Herbert, Roger, Kenelm
John, Gwladys, Teresa, Kenelm David, Jerome
Joseph, Clare, Francis, Mary Elizabeth,
Bernard, Reginald, Margaret, and John

"The harvest is abundant but the laborers are few; so ask the master of the harvest to send out laborers for his harvest" (Mt 9:37–38). Eliza Vaughan took this command of Jesus seriously. She made a holy hour for vocations every day. As a result, ten of her thirteen surviving children became priests, religious sisters, and nuns.

Louisa Elizabeth (Eliza) was born in London on October 8, 1810, to John and Martha Rolls. A wealthy Protestant family, their prominence even preceded the Rolls-Royce business that would in time make their name recognized around the world. As was common in many well-to-do families, Eliza was sent to France for her education. While there, she witnessed and was impressed by the Catholic Church's effort to help the poor. She was intrigued by the sincerity of the Church, which started her pondering the possibility of converting to the Catholic Faith.

When she returned to London, she met and fell in love with Colonel John Francis Vaughan. The Vaughans were a prominent Catholic family. During the persecution of Queen Elizabeth I some two hundred years before, the Vaughan home had been a place of refuge for priests. Mass was secretly celebrated at their Courtfield estate. As a result, the family was hounded, imprisoned, and their property expropriated. After Queen Elizabeth's reign, the family returned to its place of prominence in London society.

Soon after her marriage in 1830, Eliza converted to Catholicism with the utmost zeal, despite the strong objection of her own family.

When they began their family, Eliza suggested to her husband that they offer their children back to God. He agreed. Every day, she went to Mass and spent an hour in adoration. Before Jesus in the Holy Eucharist, she would pray for a large family. God was happy to answer her prayer.

Herbert Alfred was born first. Then came Roger William

Bede. Their third son, Kenelm John, died before he was a year old. Two girls came next — Gwladys Elizabeth Filomena and Teresa Mary. Kenelm David and Jerome Joseph were followed by Claire Mary, then Francis William, Mary Elizabeth, Bernard John, and Reginald Aloysius. Margaret Mary was the last girl.

Eliza took seriously her role as the children's primary educator. The children fondly remembered their mother teaching them by "uniting spiritual and religious obligation with amusement and cheerfulness." Each day consisted of Mass, prayer, music, art, playing, and studying. Eliza would share the lives of the saints, which inspired her children to live holy lives. They also accompanied their mother on visits to the poor and the sick so that they would learn the necessity of performing works of charity. She wanted her children to be well-rounded Catholics; she wanted them to be saints.

This mother also wished that God would call some of her children to religious and priestly life. Prayers for vocations were a large part of her daily holy hour. Imagine her delight when Herbert declared to his parents his desire to become a priest! God was answering her prayers, even though Colonel Vaughan had Herbert pegged as an excellent candidate to be a military officer. Still, the parents rejoiced with each announcement from their children that they planned to follow Jesus more closely as priests or religious.

The fourteenth and final child, John Stephen, was born on January 24, 1853. Eliza, now forty-two years old, did not survive childbirth. With sorrow in their hearts, mixed with confidence in God's love, John and the children buried Eliza on the family grounds at Courtfield.

John and Eliza's son Herbert went on to become archbishop of Westminster. He was eventually named cardinal. Roger became Archbishop of Sydney, Australia. Kenelm became a diocesan priest. Jerome Joseph entered the Benedictines and eventually became prior; he later founded Saint Benedict's Abbey at Fort Augustus, Scotland. Bernard, who had the reputation for being the most lively of all the children, became a Jesuit priest, world-renowned preacher, and author. The youngest, John, was ordained by his eldest brother and eventually became bishop of Salford. Francis and Reginald married and gave grandchildren to John and heirs to the Rolls name.

Not to be outdone by their brothers, the girls also answered Jesus' call to follow him. Four sisters entered four different convents: Gwladys became a Visitation sister in France; Teresa became Sister Helen Mary as a Daughter of Charity of Saint Vincent de Paul; Clare became a Poor Clare, of course; Mary Elizabeth, whose religious name was Sister Claire Magdalen, joined an Augustinian convent and became prioress of Saint Augustine Priory. Margaret wanted to become a religious, too, but her frail health prevented her from entering a convent. All five girls led quiet, holy lives.

These religious vocations — two religious priests, one diocesan priest, one bishop, one archbishop, one cardinal, and four nuns — were the fruit of Eliza's daily adoration and prayers. In Eliza Vaughan, biological motherhood and spiritual motherhood came together to greatly enrich the Church.

ENCOURAGING VOCATIONS

"What do you want to be when you grow up?" There are so many opportunities for our children today. Police officer, fire fighter, doctor, veterinarian, architect, athlete — the list goes on and on. Do we remember to include priests and religious brothers, sisters, or nuns in that list? We should. As Catholic parents, we need to plant the seeds of a possible religious vocation early in our children. We are also responsible for watering that seed with our prayers. We must help our children understand that God may call them to a life of service to his family, the Church.

As our children get older, the question "What do you want to be when you grow up?" should shift a bit and become, "What does God want you to be?" As Eliza Vaughan understood, our children's true happiness lies in fulfilling the special vocation for which God has created them. Whatever job they may do, God has a mission in mind for them that only they can complete. As parents, we ought to help guide them and pray, pray, pray for them.

Today, Courtfield, the Vaughan family home, is a retreat house. The chapel in that house where Eliza daily prayed is appropriately dedicated to Our Lady of Vocations. May Our Lady of Vocations pray for religious and priestly vocations within our families.

OUR PRAYER

Father in heaven, thank you for our priests, religious brothers, sisters, and nuns. Bless them for their life of service to us and their dedication to our spiritual well-being. The world needs more of them. Indeed, the harvest is ready, but the laborers are few. If it pleases you, Lord, choose from among our children the laborers you send into your vineyard. Through the intercession of Eliza Vaughan, grant our Church an increase of good, holy vocations. We ask this through Jesus Christ, the master of the harvest. Amen.

Ven. Margaret Bosco

FAST FACTS

April 1, 1788–November 25, 1856

Feast day: November 25

Patron of foster children

Children: Three — Anthony (stepson),
Joseph, and St. John Bosco

Have you ever been so tired that you felt you just could not accomplish one more task? It is amazing all we can do with God's good grace. Ven. Margaret Bosco is a wonderful example of someone who continued to do great things for the Lord beyond what even she thought she had the energy to do.

Margaret Occhiena was the sixth of ten children born to a pious, poor family. Many of her siblings died young. Margaret had no formal education, yet she was wise beyond her years. Though illiterate, she memorized her catechism and listened attentively at church to the readings and homilies. Moreover, she always made time at the beginning of her day to pray and then continued the conversation with God throughout the day. This was the source of her wisdom.

When Francesco Bosco asked Margaret Occhiena to marry him, she said, "No!" The twenty-seven-year-old Bosco was already a widower with a son and a semiparalyzed mother for whom to care. Margaret, however, had her own aging parents who needed her. Lovingly, Margaret's siblings stepped in and promised to watch over their parents, and her father gave his blessing. The twenty-four-year-old Margaret was free to marry Francesco. By the age of twenty-nine, she was a widow with an ailing mother-in-law, a stepson, and two young sons of her own.

Margaret raised all three boys, Anthony, Joseph, and John, to be hard workers. She made sure they knew their catechism and lived their faith. She was strict, but the boys knew she loved them dearly. Together, they made a modest living on their farm.

Mama Margaret may have been the first mother to tell her children to "Offer it up!" From a young age, this was a practice she herself embraced. She would offer difficult farm tasks or monotonous family work for others to the glory of God. If she had a particularly difficult day, she asked Jesus to take it and turn it into something good for someone whose circumstance was worse than her own. She taught her boys to do the same. Despite their poverty, the little family considered themselves blessed.

When the youngest son, John, was nine, he told his mother about a dream he had in which some rowdy boys were fighting him. Then, Jesus and Mary appeared in his dream. Jesus told John that fighting them would not change the boys' hearts. At a wave of his hand, the boys turned into wild animals. Next, Our Lady waved her hand, and the wild animals became lambs. Margaret understood from this dream that God had a special mission in mind for John. From that day on, she did her best to make sure that John had the education he needed to become a priest.

June 5, 1841, the day John was ordained, was one of the happiest days in Margaret's life. She knew what a blessing it is to have a son who is a priest. She also understood the responsibility he bore. She told him, "To see you dressed in this manner fills my heart with joy. But remember that it is not the dress that gives honor to the state, but the practice of virtue. If at any time you come to doubt your vocation, I beseech you, lay it aside at once. I would rather have a poor peasant for my son than a negligent priest." She did not have to worry; John would go on to become a saintly priest, and she would have a role to play in his ministry.

At the age of fifty-eight, Margaret's hard life eased up a good bit. She was enjoying the joyful life of doting grandmother. Between Anthony and Joseph, she had nine beautiful grandchildren. A model of faith and love, she graced their lives; a source of joy and pleasure, they graced hers.

Then Don (the title for priest in Italian) Bosco became seriously ill and was sent home to recover. His unending ministry to the poor boys in the city of Turin had taken a toll on him, and he needed rest. Being with his mama gave Don Bosco the physical and spiritual strength he needed to return. The question remained, however, about his ability to continue his ministry without getting worn out again. His solution was to ask his mother to join him in taking care of his boys. "If you believe this to be the will of the Lord, I am ready to go," she replied. So Margaret left her calm rural life for hectic city life.

Mama Margaret, as the boys called her, quickly became a surrogate mother to the orphans that lived in the home Don Bosco had established for them. She tended a garden, grew vegetables, and cooked meals for them, washed and mended their clothes, and taught them how to keep their home clean. Her presence turned what Don Bosco called the Oratory into a real home and family for these boys.

When the boys at the Oratory praised Don Bosco for his virtues, they often summed up their compliment by saying, "He got it from Mama Margaret." What a tribute! And what a goal for us as mothers, to have others recognize the virtues in our children and to know that those virtues were instilled in them by us, their mothers.

A time came when Mama Margaret felt that she had had enough. Life in the Oratory was loud, and the boys could be rough. She sat down with her son to have a heart-to-heart conversation, telling him she could do it no more. She wanted to return to the country. John listened and said nothing. When she finished speaking, his eyes wandered to the wall; her eyes followed his. They gazed upon the crucifix hanging there. Tears welled up in those loving eyes of hers. God and John were asking her to unite her sufferings with his. She stayed.

Still, John realized he had to get his mother some help. More and more volunteers began to join this ministry of nurturing, teaching, and training young boys. Before long, Don Bosco and Margaret founded the Salesian apostolate.

In an effort to provide some relief for his mother, John and Mama Margaret would take trips back home to the country. Of course, they often took some of their boys with them to expose them to the fresh country air. Such trips were always a source of comfort and joy for the whole family.

On one trip home, however, Mama Margaret became ill. A cough and fever confined her to bed. The doctor diagnosed her with pneumonia. Margaret would not return to the Oratory. John was not sure how he would continue without her; after all, the boys needed her presence. Sweetly, she reminded him, "Our Blessed Lady will always be in charge."

Margaret Occhiena Bosco died a rich woman. She had no money to her name, but the line of boys in the funeral procession to the parish church told how rich she truly was. Possessions, of which she had none, do not go with us when we die; the love that we give away while on earth, though, becomes the wings by which we ascend to heaven.

PERSEVERING THROUGH EXHAUSTION

After successfully raising three sons as a single mother, Margaret could have sat back and enjoyed her life. After all, she deserved it. Isn't that what we would say?

Yet she saw a need. Her son needed her; those poor, orphaned boys in the city needed her. So instead of sitting back, she rose up to fulfill that need. She gave the last ten years of her life to supporting and guiding "her" boys.

Love motivates us to do that — to continue giving even when we feel exhausted and done. Then, supernatural grace takes over. God is loving through us. Jesus says to us what he said to Saint Paul: "My grace is sufficient for you, for power is made perfect in weakness" (2 Cor 12:9). When, like Mama Margaret, you have had enough and you cannot do any more, look to the cross to receive your strength.

Now, that is not to say that we can never take time for ourselves. St. John Bosco took his mother to the countryside for a break when needed. Even Jesus retreated to pray and be alone with his Father. We, too, will need a mommy timeout on occasion. Try to take time for yourself during the day, even if it is just half an hour in the morning, or during afternoon nap time, or at night after the children go to bed. Do something for yourself — sit, relax, watch TV, or read a book. Going on an occasional retreat can also be rejuvenating. Do not feel guilty leaving the children for a day with Dad or Grandma. Grab a mommy girlfriend and go! You will return refreshed.

One last piece of advice — something I learned the hard way. Children demand a lot of our time, but do not forget your husband. Make time for him. If possible, schedule monthly date nights. Even if money is tight, you two can still go on a walk, hike, or ride around town. Picnics are nice, too. Put aside being mommy and daddy for a little while and just be a couple again.

Remember, love is never divided; it can only multiply. God, who is infinite, is love. And he is always available to help us spread his love. As Ven. Margaret Bosco reveals, mothers have a lot of love to share.

OUR PRAYER

Heavenly Father, your love and providence are reflected in family life. We praise you for the blessings you constantly bestow on our families. Keep us strong and united to you. We ask your blessings on broken families, on children in foster care, and on children in need of a loving family through adoption. Make broken families whole again, and through the intercession of Ven. Margaret Bosco, let no child go through this life feeling unloved. We ask this in the loving Heart of Jesus. Amen.

St. Zélie Martin

FAST FACTS
December 23, 1831–August 28, 1877

Feast day: July 12

Patron saint of breast cancer patients, marriages

Children: Nine — Marie Louise, Marie Pauline, Marie
Léonie, Marie Hélène, Joseph Louis, Joseph Jean-
Baptiste, Marie Céline, Marie Mélanie-Thérèse, and
Marie Françoise-Thérèse (St. Thérèse of Lisieux)

While I was battling morning sickness with my sixth child, my mother was battling breast cancer. The grace, courage, and humor with which she persevered were awe-inspiring. I think I complained more about the nausea and being tired than she ever did about her cancer. Her example reminded me of another holy mommy.

Marie-Azélie Guérin wanted to be a nun, but poor health precluded her from religious life. She accepted this disappointment as God's will. When she met Louis Martin at the age of twenty-seven, she was already a successful businesswoman as one of the city of Alençon's most talented lace makers. Like Zélie, Louis's hopes of becoming a religious had been thwarted. Drawn to his piety and love of the Lord, Zélie accepted Louis's marriage proposal, and they were married just three months later.

Their confessor discouraged their original intention of living as celibates. Upon receiving his counsel, the couple decided to raise as many children as possible for the glory of God. The family grew to include nine children, although four died young.

When a mother loses a child, her heart breaks. Yet for Zélie her sorrow was mixed with joy: "When I had to close the eyes of my dear children and bury them, I felt deep sorrow, but I was always resigned to it. ... I do not think that the sorrows and the troubles endured could possibly be compared with the eternal happiness of my children with God. Besides, they are not lost to me forever; life is short and filled with crosses, and we shall find them again in heaven." The thought of having children safe in heaven gave their mother great comfort.

Furthermore, Zélie taught her children to pray to their "baby saints." When little Hélène was suddenly cured of an inner ear inflammation, Zélie attributed it to the prayers of baby Joseph before the throne of Jesus. Though in heaven, Joseph Louis, Joseph Jean-Baptiste, Melanie, and eventually Hélène were still very much part of the family.

Crosses seemed to be ever-present in Zélie's l... of being rejected for religious life, the cross of the death of four children within three years, the cross of ill health. This last cross climaxed when a lump under her arm, the result of an injury eleven years previous, became swollen and painful. The doctor told her the lump was a cancerous tumor; it was incurable. With this news, Zélie abandoned herself to God's will and consoled her husband and daughters.

Abandonment to God's will does not mean abandonment of hope. Zélie admitted that, from the bottom of her heart, she wanted to live. She prayed that she not be taken from this world as long as her children needed her. Despite the pain, she continued her ordinary life.

As the disease progressed, the family decided that their mother ought to make a pilgrimage to Lourdes. Her love and devotion to Mary gave her every reason to trust that she would receive the miracle for which her family so ardently hoped. It was, however, not to be. If anything, Zélie came back from her pilgrimage weakened and worse. Yet she returned as cheerfully as if she had obtained the hoped-for miracle.

Zélie trusted Our Lady to obtain what was best for her. Such was her devotion to Mary that she made a shrine in her home for a large Marian statue. This shrine was so beautiful that her daughters joked that it rivaled the one at their parish church. Their mother would place fancy lace over a blue fabric background and adorn it with fresh flowers from the countryside. Often, these bouquets would reach the ceiling. In a way, the beautiful flowers represented Zélie's abundant love for Our Lady. She trusted that, if it was God's will that she leave this world, our Blessed Mother would take care of the children left behind.

As time progressed, so did the cancer. With her arm practically paralyzed, she could no longer dress herself or write her letters. Her last letter was a few lines scribbled to her brother:

"What can be done? If the Blessed Virgin does not cure me, that means my time here is at an end, and the good God wishes me to rest elsewhere than upon this earth." Her body was weak, but her soul was strong. She submitted to God's will. She was going to be reunited with her children in heaven. This thought gave great comfort to her sorrowing husband and daughters upon Zélie's death.

****

Zélie Martin left us with so many of her letters that we get an unusually personal and close look into her struggles and feelings.

During Lent one year, she wrote to her daughter Pauline about her efforts to fast: "Only 21 days more, but 21 days that pass by slowly, for we must carry out our Lenten regulations. It is so tiring! How I long for Easter!" I feel her pain! But mine comes from just trying to restrain myself from eating chocolate and drinking coffee. Zélie full-out fasted and abstained all forty days of Lent!

In another letter, she once confided to a friend, "It is over little things that I worry most." I get her! She worried about bringing in enough money from her business to justly compensate her working women. Sometimes I worry about paying bills. Yet God always provides, in the big and little things.

Finally, like all mothers, she worried about her children. She was especially concerned about Thérèse's strong will and Léonie's constant tantrums. You know the cool thing about this? Thérèse is, of course, a great saint and Doctor of the Church, and Léonie's cause for canonization has begun! A mother's persistent prayers and God's wonderful grace can fix anything.

Like St. Zélie Martin always did, we can cease worrying and keep praying. God is worthy of our trust.

THE CROSS OF ILLNESSES

Cancer is a scary thing. I think we all know someone who has been affected by this disease. My mother is a breast cancer survivor. Praise God that technology and treatment has come such a long way since Saint Zélie's time.

Many mothers carry the cross of chronic or even terminal illness. Just to be feeling sick for a few days can make mothering more difficult. At these times, we must rely on God's own strength to get us through the illness.

I asked my mother what advice she would give to those who have been diagnosed with cancer or any serious illness. Here are the four things that most helped her get through her treatments:

1. **Prayer!** In prayer you will find strength, comfort, and resolve.
2. **A reason to fight.** Children and/or grandchildren are big reasons. Being specific may help make your purpose more concrete. For example, "I want to see my child cross the stage at graduation" or "I want to hold my first grandbaby."
3. **A promised reward for getting through treatment.** My father took my mother on a cruise to Alaska. It does not have to be that elaborate, but it should be something you will definitely look forward to.
4. **Good, positive people — family, friends, doctors.** I fondly remember my mother's two Jewish friends who would come to visit her a couple days after her treatment. They would get her out of bed and take her somewhere. My mother resisted sometimes, saying she was tired, which I am sure she was. Yet she always returned from these little trips rejuvenated.

My mother survived breast cancer and all its nasty treatments.

My sixth child, a daughter, is named Catherine after my mom. Mom missed Cate's baptism because she was in the hospital with the pneumonia she contracted while going through chemotherapy; however, she has not missed a birthday party, First Communion, or any of my children's other special occasions since. My mom is the strongest woman I know.

For those of you struggling with illness, or worrying about a friend or family member with cancer, pray to St. Zélie Martin. She knows what you are going through — your thoughts, your fears, your hopes. Ask her daughter, Saint Thérèse, to join her mother in praying before the throne of Jesus for your cure. Be at peace and trust the answer will come.

OUR PRAYER

Heavenly Father, your will is always for our good, and you can bring good even out of our sufferings. Strengthen us and increase our trust. Through the intercession of St. Zélie Martin, give strength and courage to mothers battling cancer or other diseases. May our hope always rest in you. We ask this through Jesus Christ, our reason for hope. Amen.

Bl. Marianna Biernacka

FAST FACTS
1888–June 13, 1943

Memorial: June 12, as one of the 108
Polish martyrs of World War II

Patron of mothers-in-law

Children: Six, two who survived past
infancy — Leokadia and Stanislaw

W hat would your reaction be if your husband came home one day and announced that his mother would be moving in with you? Would you consider it a blessing or a nightmare? Stanislaw Biernacka found himself having to share this news with his young wife, Anna. His father, Ludwik Biernacka, had passed away; his mother, Marianna, was unable to keep their little farm going on her own. Stanislaw's sister, Leokadia, had married and moved away to the city with her husband. Isn't that how it usually goes? So Marianna moved in with her son and his wife.

Now, Marianna was one of those mothers-in-law who was a joy to have in the home. A noncomplaining, hard-working woman, Marianna had always shared with her husband the backbreaking work of cultivating the family farm to yield a sustaining crop. In the winter, when the farm was dormant, Marianna could be found spinning and weaving at the loom. Her daughter-in-law, Anna, a farm girl herself, could appreciate her mother-in-law's industriousness and welcomed the help on their farm and in her kitchen.

When Anna gave birth to a girl, Eugenia, Marianna was thrilled. The grandmother helped bring up the child by example and in deed. Just as she had done when Stanislaw was a child, Marianna sang devotional songs to her granddaughter. She prayed with her and for her. What a joy it was to Marianna to be such a big part of Genia's life.

The simple yet happy life of the Beirnacka family changed, however, when Hitler's army invaded Poland on September 1, 1939. Under German occupation, all Poles were stripped of their rights. The Polish language was banned. Churches, as well as bookstores and libraries, were ransacked and burned. Priests were rounded up and sent to concentration camps. Many men were conscripted into military service. All food was rationed. These were sad and difficult times. Still, the little family withstood the hardships by trusting in the Lord.

Graces received from years of praying the Rosary and Divine Office, attending many Masses, and performing works of mercy were brought to fruition for Marianna on the day the Nazis came banging on the door. Apparently, a soldier had been shot and killed in a nearby town by a member of a resistance group. The soldiers were there to arrest Stanislaw and Anna, even though the Nazis did not judge the couple as having anything to do with the shooting, or even with the resistance itself. Still, the practice was to round up and execute ten people for every one soldier who was taken out by the resistance. Stanislaw and Anna just happened to be randomly selected.

Marianna pleaded with soldiers. "I will go for her! Let me go," she cried out. Marianna placed herself between the soldiers and her eight-months-pregnant daughter-in-law, begging to be taken instead. On her knees, she pointed to Anna's belly indicating that they would be taking an extra prisoner by apprehending this pregnant woman. Likewise, she asked that they consider the welfare of the frightened toddler before them.

The soldiers were undoubtedly moved by her pleas. As long as they filled their quota, they really didn't care whom they arrested. So they grabbed Marianna and her son Stanislaw and left the home, leaving Anna and her two-year-old daughter behind.

For two weeks, Marianna, Stanislaw, and others were held in a prison at Grodno, Belarus. During that time, Marianna prayed her rosary, which she had with her at the time of her arrest. Then, on June 13, 1943, Marianna, still with rosary in hand, was executed by firing squad. Her body was thrown into a common grave.

Soon after, Anna Beirnacka gave birth to a son, whom she named Stanislaw after his father. The child, unfortunately, lived only a year. Anna herself, however, lived to be ninety-eight. Eugenia disclosed that her mother would often say, "I have been given life twice; once by my mother and then by my mother-in-law."

Marianna Biernacka was beatified by Pope John Paul II fifty-six years after her execution. She is one of 108 martyrs from World War II, all Polish: three bishops, fifty-two priests, twenty-six male religious, eighteen female religious, and eight other laypeople. In total, it is estimated that eleven million people were victims of the Holocaust. Three million were Catholic or Christian Poles. Among them was this self-sacrificing woman who loved her daughter-in-law and grandchildren more than life itself.

THE SACRIFICES OF MOTHERHOOD

"I have been crucified with Christ; yet I live, no longer I, but Christ lives in me" (Gal 2:19–20). Moms really feel this verse. If it were not for Jesus, we might not make it through some days, or nights! It is true, of course — our lives are not our own. Once we become mothers, we live for the family.

Being a mom means making sacrifices. We probably will not be called upon to make the ultimate sacrifice, as Blessed Marianna was; however, we make many little sacrifices every day. Taking our children to their activities instead of going where we would like to go; listening to "Wheels on the Bus" for the umpteenth time and not our own playlist; staying up with a sick child, costing us some much-needed sleep; these are only a few ways we put our families before ourselves. When these acts are done for love of our families and God, they can make us holy.

So we should not feel sorry for ourselves (though some days we may be tempted to do so). We make these sacrifices willingly. Our goal is to serve our family out of love with a joyful heart. It is not always easy, but we continue to serve. It is what we are called to do.

Blessed Marianna's ultimate sacrifice began with doing the little things — working the farm throughout the hot days of summer, spinning and weaving during the dark days of winter, helping her husband in whatever way she was needed, and raising her children the best she could. When she moved in with her son, she helped her daughter-in-law with the housework and watched over her granddaughter. Most importantly, her work was balanced and sanctified by prayer.

Blessed Marianna had a heart that was willing to give of self. A lifetime of prayer and sacrifice enabled her on that fateful day to totally give her life for her daughter-in-law and grandbabies. Though not to this extent, every day we are faced with opportunities to form a heart of selfless giving. Daily sacrifices help us become more like Christ.

Speaking of sacrifices, keep in mind that our mothers-in-law have made sacrifices that have benefited us. After years of raising their beloved sons, they give them up. While it is only natural that children grow up and move away from home, a mother's heart feels a twinge when the time comes to let go.

So do your best to love and respect your mother-in-law, even if you do not have one as wonderful as Blessed Marianna. Keep her posted on your lives; at least have your husband call regularly to talk with her. You may endear yourself to her if occasionally you ask for her advice. If she makes any rude comments, ignore them. In this way, you will be like Christ, who "submitted / and did not open his mouth" (Is 53:7). Remember to always pray and thank God for your mother-in-law, for without her, you very well could still be single!

And if you are a mother-in-law, love and respect your daughter-in-law. Find ways to compliment her and keep suggestions to yourself unless asked. Strive to be helpful, as Bl. Marianna Biernacka was. Likewise, pray and thank God for your daughter-in-law, for she makes your son happy and perhaps has made (or will make) you a grandmother.

A mother's life is one of sacrificial love. Not just for our children do we make sacrifices, but for the whole family. Moreover, our love flows out to our extended families and even to the whole family of God. After all, we do it all for the love of Christ, who made the ultimate sacrifice for us.

OUR PRAYER

Father and Creator of all, thank you for our mothers-in-law. Through them, we have been blessed with the precious gift of our husbands. Through the intercession of Blessed Marianna, may we make the sacrifices asked of us with love and joy. We ask this through Jesus Christ, who made the greatest sacrifice of all for us. Amen.

Bl. Maria Corsini-Beltrame Quattrocchi

FAST FACTS
June 24, 1884–August 26, 1965

Feast day: November 25

Patron (along with her husband) of married couples

Children: Four — Filippo, Stefania,
Cesare, and Enrichetta

Have you ever seen an elderly couple shuffling down the street or in a store hand in hand and thought, "Life Goal! Please, God, let that be me and my husband one day." That couple is epitomized in Luigi and Maria Beltarme Quattrocchi, the first couple to be beatified together. Theirs was a marriage of true mutual sanctification.

Maria Corsini first met Luigi, the son of a family friend, at her family's home in Florence. He was a lawyer, having received his law degree from the distinguished La Sapienza University in Rome. He was good-looking and smart. Moreover, the young man already had a reputation for being diligent and honest. He would make a wonderful husband, Maria thought.

Maria, too, was beautiful and intelligent. Much of Maria's beauty shone from the inside out. From a young age she developed the habit of going to daily Mass and saying the Rosary. Prayer and charity were an integral part of who she was. After graduation from college, she became a professor of education and, in time, a sought-after lecturer and author.

On November 25, 1905, the couple was married at the Basilica of Mary Major in Rome. Sounds like a match made in heaven, doesn't it? Though an honest and unselfish man, Luigi did not have a strong faith. Once married to Maria, however, that began to change. He attended daily Mass with her and grew in Christian virtue. In their marriage, one saw true mutual sanctification at work.

Open to the gift of life, Maria and Luigi had three children in the first four years of their marriage. First a son, Filippo, was born to them, followed by a girl, Stefania, then another boy, Cesare. In 1913, while pregnant with her fourth child, Maria was diagnosed with placenta previa. Doctors urged her to terminate the pregnancy, giving her only a 5 percent chance of living through the pregnancy and delivery. The mother vehemently declined the abortion; Luigi agreed. Heartlessly, the doctors told

Luigi to expect to be a widower with three young children then. Nonetheless, the couple, having already consecrated their family to the Sacred Heart of Jesus, would trust in him.

The pregnancy was a rough one, on both Maria and Luigi. While Maria suffered the side effects of a difficult pregnancy, Luigi worried about losing his wife. When Luigi sorrowfully shared his concerns with the parish priest, Father encouraged him to continue to trust in the Lord. Beyond all human hope, on April 6, 1914, the mother delivered a healthy baby girl, Enrichetta, without any complications to mother or baby.

Deepened in faith, the couple raised their family with many of the devotions of the Catholic Church. A portrait of the Sacred Heart of Jesus was displayed prominently in the family parlor. The family faithfully made First Friday holy hours, attended daily Mass, and recited the Rosary together every evening. Maria exhibited everyday holiness in performing ordinary household tasks and carrying out her maternal responsibilities.

Their devout family life manifested itself in visible actions. With their children in tow, Maria and Luigi started scouting groups in the poorer neighborhoods of Rome. Maria was a part of the General Council of the Italian Catholic Women's Association and was active in the Women's Catholic Action group. With Luigi, she founded UNITALSI, an organization that assists infirm and handicapped people on pilgrimages to Lourdes and other holy sites. At home, the door to her house was always open to friends as well as those seeking food or help. Maria was a model of generosity.

When World War II broke out, Maria volunteered as a nurse for the Italian Red Cross. As she had always done, she opened her home to those in need, including Jewish refugees. She did what she could to alleviate the sufferings caused by the war.

Inspired by their parents' virtues of piety and generosity, three of their four children offered their lives in service to the

Church. Filippo became a Benedictine priest, Stefania a Benedictine nun, and Cesare a Trappist monk. Enrichetta remained home and was a blessing to her parents in their later years. In 1951, Maria's beloved Luigi died suddenly of a heart attack. Blessed Maria lived another fourteen years before dying peacefully in Enrichetta's arms.

On October 21, 2001, Pope St. John Paul II fulfilled a desire he had — to beatify a married couple in recognition of how married men and women lead holy lives through their vocation. That couple of extraordinary holiness in ordinary life was Maria and Luigi Beltrame Quattrocchi.

OUR BUSY SCHEDULES

Bl. Maria Corsini was one busy mom. Many of us can totally identify with feeling stretched beyond our limits. When feeling overwhelmed, we need to examine the things that keep us moving. Those things that occupy most of our time clearly indicate what we consider most important — even if we don't fully realize it. Likewise, what we put on our children's schedules tells them what we think should be important for them.

When Jesus reveals the greatest commandments — love God with all your heart, mind, soul, and strength, and love your neighbor as yourself (see Mt 22:37–39) — he is pointing out what our priorities ought to be. Our time should be spent loving God and others.

Maria Corsini offers us a helpful model and guide as we consider our own priorities. Do we take time to love God each day? The Church offers us a treasury of devotions to show our love for God and put him first in our lives. Take advantage of these gifts: Mass, the Rosary, the Divine Office, holy hours, adoration, consecration to the Sacred Heart, consecration to Mary, the communion of saints, the Divine Mercy chaplet, and a plethora of prayers. There are so many ways to share in the life of God himself.

Bl. Maria Corsini also reminds us of the importance of serving others. Do our children see us loving our neighbor? Do we encourage them to love others? Service should not be measured in required hours for Confirmation or graduation; it must become part of who we are. Visiting nursing homes, serving at soup kitchens, preparing meals for the sick, and befriending a homebound senior are just a few examples of how we may be called to step out of our comfort zone to show love for others. Buying supplies and giving financially are important, too, but they cannot replace hands-on participation in service.

Life is busy; life with children is even busier. Following the example of Maria Corsini, choose carefully what is going to occupy your time.

OUR PRAYER

Heavenly Father, praise be to you for the sacraments, sacramentals, and devotions you have given to the Church to draw us closer to you. Help us to use these gifts. Then, armed with the graces we receive, inspire us to serve others and show them your love. Through the intercession of Bl. Maria Corsini-Beltrame Quattrocchi, may we always be busy loving you with all our heart, mind, soul, and strength, and our neighbors as ourselves. We ask this through Jesus Christ, our example. Amen.

St. Gianna Molla

FAST FACTS

October 4, 1922–April 28, 1962

Feast day: April 28

Patron saint of unborn children and physicians

Children: Four — Pierluigi, Maria Zita,
Laura, and Gianna Emanuela

Heroes and heroines are known for the one, big, brave act that they perform. Oftentimes, though, that brave act is the summation of many little acts of love. Such is the case with St. Gianna Beretta Molla. While she is known for the decision she made to save her baby's life at the cost of her own, that decision was only possible after living a life of trust in God and sacrifice for others.

Gianna was the tenth of thirteen children. Imagine the many sacrifices that were made daily in her childhood home, just in bathroom use alone! Hers was a strong Catholic family that produced a priest, a nun, and a saint. On the outside, Gianna was like any of us. She enjoyed music, painting, hiking, and skiing. Her loving heart led her to become an active member in the St. Vincent de Paul Society and a leader in the Catholic Action movement. She was also a diligent student and went to the university to become a pediatric physician.

Originally, she planned to join her brother in the mission fields of Brazil. She yearned to tend to the poor of that country and share God's love for them, body and soul. Our plans, however, are not always God's plans. Chronic health problems prevented her from being able to join her missionary brother. Finally, her confessor urged her to accept that God's will for her was in marriage.

Good thing her future husband, Pietro Molla, did not know that she had intentions of being a missionary, or else he admitted may never have approached her. While attending the first Mass of a mutual friend who was newly ordained, Pietro and Gianna officially met. I say officially, because Dr. Gianna Beretta had been the attending doctor who comforted Pietro's sister as she lay dying in the hospital years earlier. He saw her again when he went to her brother's doctor's office for treatment of his own ailment. So he had had his eye on her for a while before he got up the courage to introduce himself. Their first date was to a ballet on New Year's Eve 1954. In February, Gianna wrote Pietro a note: "I must tell you right away that I am a woman who wants affection very much; I have found you, and I intend to give myself totally in order to form a truly Christian family." Thus, at her suggestion, their engagement began with Mass and Holy Communion, after she received her beautiful ring in April that year. Gianna, likewise, encouraged Pietro to make a triduum (a three-day religious observance) with her during the three days before their wedding on September 24, which he gladly did, though he admits he would never have thought of it himself.

Pietro and Gianna had three children in four years — Pierluigi, Maria Zita (whom they called Mariolina), and Laura. Gianna also suffered two miscarriages. After the births of her children, she would give money from her savings to the missions in thanksgiving to God for entrusting a precious child to her and her husband. Gianna viewed life as a beautiful gift from God.

Gianna was able to balance her life as wife, mother, and doctor. As with many of our mommy saints, her day began with Mass and prayer. Her doctor's office was her mission field, where she treated children, their mothers, and the elderly, for whom she had a tender spot in her heart. Her love for children made her want to have a large family.

In the second month of her sixth pregnancy, Gianna experienced unimaginable pain in her lower abdomen. A fibroma tumor was discovered on her uterus. The doctors gave her three choices: (1) abort the baby and begin treatment of the tumor, and she would still possibly be able to have children in the future; (2) have a total hysterectomy, which would assuredly save her life but end the baby's; (3) surgically remove the tumor, which could protect her baby's life but cause risk to her own. Gianna would not even consider the first option because she knew that purposefully killing her child was a mortal sin. The second option was allowed in the eyes of the Church. Although the hysterectomy would cause the unborn baby's death, the intended effect was to save the mother's life, not to terminate the pregnancy, and not performing the surgery could result in the death of both mother and baby. However, wanting to protect the life of her unborn child, Gianna opted for the third surgery.

The tumor was successfully removed during surgery, and baby did well. The operation, however, caused complications throughout the remaining pregnancy. Through it all, Gianna continued her duties as mother, wife, and doctor. She did not let on how much suffering she was experiencing. Saint Gianna would often say, "One cannot love without suffering or suffer without loving." She lived by this motto.

Finally, the day of the Caesarian section to deliver her baby girl arrived. Gianna did not want to die; she wanted to be a wife to her husband and a mother to her children. Being a doctor, however, she understood the risks — that she or the baby could die. She told Pietro, "This time, it will be a difficult delivery, and they may have to save one or the other — I want them to save my baby." God answered Gianna's prayers: A healthy baby girl, named after her mother, was born.

Post-operative complications, unfortunately, caused an infection in the mother. She became very sick and fell into a coma. Her husband remained at her side. At one point, she awakened. She told Pietro that she had been to "the other side." She smiled and asked him, "Do you know what I saw there? I will tell you — soon." Her revelation was not to be given to Pietro in this life, though. Seven days after giving birth to a beautiful baby girl, thirty-nine-year-old Gianna Molla passed to the other side.

Gianna Emanuela, the baby for whom Saint Gianna gave her life, grew up to become a doctor herself. While her mother was a pediatrician, Doctor Gianna Emanuela is a geriatrician. Thus, mother and daughter, by their very professions, witness to the dignity and sanctity of life from beginning to end.

Doctor Gianna Emanuela now works full time at the Saint Gianna Foundation. She travels the world speaking about her parents' love and their acceptance of the crosses in their lives. She encourages people to say "Yes" to God, even when they don't understand. Moreover, she is honored to meet children from all around the world named after her mother and couples who pray to her mother. Encouraging the people she meets to love with all they have, Doctor Gianna often states, "I would not be here if I was not loved so much."

Doctor Gianna Emanuela was present at her mother's canonization, along with her father and her siblings. It was the first time in Church history that a husband attended the canonization of his wife.

MOTHERS IN THE COMMUNION OF SAINTS

Why did God allow Bl. Maria Corsini to deliver a healthy baby and remain healthy herself, but not St. Gianna Molla? Why did he not answer the prayers of the faith-filled Martin family and give Zélie the miracle of a cure for which she and her family so ardently hoped? How hard it is when God does not answer our prayers in the way we desire. We know that God can make a miracle happen and believe that he will, but then he doesn't. Why? It is a mystery. Who can know the mind of God or understand his ways (see 1 Cor 2:16)?

My aunt was diagnosed with lung cancer. While hopes that she would survive the dreaded disease waxed and waned, I was confident in one thing — God would let her see her granddaughter, the fruit of her many prayers, the answer to many lit candles. You see, after years struggling with infertility, my cousin and his wife were finally expecting a baby. They were due in October; my aunt passed away in July. I lamented to my uncle, "I thought for sure God would let her hold that baby." The response my uncle gave me is the wisdom of a man with great faith. He said, "She *is* holding her in a way much closer than she ever could have here on earth."

What a precious gift God has given us in the communion of saints! Loved ones who die in the state of grace, though separated from us physically, are still present to us. We can talk to them still, and they, in turn, intercede face-to-face with God for us. From their privileged position, they see and know our needs even better than we do. With their work on earth ended (and any necessary purification in purgatory completed), they ecstatically await the day when we will join them in heaven. Because of Jesus' sacrificial love for us, death has lost its victory, and its sting is only temporary. What comfort it is to know they are in perfect peace and happiness with Our Lord!

The thought of being reunited with loved ones brings us great joy. The separation can seem like a long time, yet compared to eternity, our time apart is just a tiny fraction of a millisecond.

Until then, be assured that moms in heaven still guide us, pray for us, and, if you pay really close attention, still give us signs of their love for us. Like the Blessed Mother, until all are safely home, a mother's job is never quite done.

OUR PRAYER

Heavenly Father, praise be to you for loving us so much that you sacrificed your only begotten Son so that we might one day join you on the "other side" in paradise. While on this side, Lord, help us to perform those small, heroic acts of selflessness for love of you and our families. And when things happen that we just don't understand, let us trust in your love for us. Through the intercession of Saint Gianna, may we truly value every life from conception to natural death and inspire others to do the same. We ask this through Jesus Christ, the giver of all life. Amen.

Sources

Bessieres, Albert. *Wife, Mother, and Mystic: Blessed Anna-Maria Taigi.* Translated by Stephen Rigby. Charlotte: Tan Books, 1952.

Emmerich, Anne Catherine. *The Life of the Blessed Virgin Mary.* Translated by Michael Palairet. Charlotte: Tan Books, 2004.

Hendey, Lisa M. *A Book of Saints for Catholic Moms.* Notre Dame: Ave Maria Press, 2011.

Martin, Celine. *The Mother of the Little Flower.* Rockford: Tan Books, 2005.

Molla, Pietro, and Elio Guerriero. *Saint Gianna Molla: Wife, Mother, Doctor.* San Francisco: Ignatius Press, 2004.

Musurillo, Herbert, trans. "The Martyrdom of Saints Perpetua and

Felicitas." In *The Acts of the Christian Martyrs*. Oxford University Press, 1972. Accessed on PBS *Frontline*.

O'Donnell, Catherine. *Elizabeth Seton: American Saint*. Ithaca, NY: Cornell University Press, 2018.

Walker, Alexander, trans. *Protoevangelium of James*. In *Ante-Nicene Fathers*, Vol. 8. Edited by Alexander Roberts, James Donaldson, and A. Cleveland Coxe. Buffalo, NY: Christian Literature Publishing Co., 1886. Revised and edited for New Advent by Kevin Knight. http://www.newadvent.org/fathers/0847.htm.

Acknowledgments

Writing this book was something I wanted to do for a long time. I wasn't sure that getting it published and sharing it with you would ever happen. I praise God for making my dream come true.

I would like to thank Lisa Hendey, creator of CatholicMom .com and author. After I read her book, *A Book of Saints for Catholic Moms,* I contacted her, telling her of my desire to one day write a book solely about saints who were mothers and asking for advice. She graciously responded to my email with an offer to write for CatholicMom.com. This opportunity has enabled me to find my voice, hone my writing skills, and engage with a larger Catholic audience. Thank you, Lisa, for allowing me to be a part of the CatholicMom.com family.

Thank you, Barbara Szyszkiewicz, for sending out that email informing me that Our Sunday Visitor was looking for new book ideas. As editor of CatholicMom.com, you have done so much to encourage and support me. God bless you for all you do for me and CatholicMom.

A hearty caffeinated thank you to Sarah Reinhard, my acquisitions editor, for being so excited about this idea and guiding me in my first steps in writing this book.

Mary Beth Baker, my wonderful editor, I appreciate you answering my many questions and working with me until *Saintly Moms* was just right for our readers.

My dear friend, Laura Wolf, I cannot thank you enough for marking up my first draft, catching many mistakes, and making my writing clearer. God bless you for taking time to proofread my book.

A special thank you to my pastor, Father Michael Roach, who read each chapter in its rawest form, pointed out my split infinitives and other grammatical errors, added some quotes and fun facts, and encouraged me to keep writing.

I must thank my parents, Richard and Cookie Hauf. Dad and Mom, even before the thought of writing a book ever popped into my head, you believed in my writing skills. Ever since I wrote to you from the convent, you recognized that I had a desire to share our Faith with others, and you emboldened me to do it through the written word, as well as in spoken word and action. Thank you for the gift of Faith — the greatest gift you have ever given me.

I should also acknowledge my four youngest children, Cate, Barbara, Leah, and Peter. I homeschool until high school; thus, these four often had the assignment for religion class to find the facts about some of the saints in this book. Thank you, little ones, for all your help. Thanks to all my children for always loving me and being patient with me. I love you more than words can say.

Speaking of love — to the love of my life, Paul. Thank you so much for championing me in my effort to write this book. Through you, God blessed me with ten wonderful children. Together, we are raising them to know, love, and serve the Lord. Thank you for helping me in my efforts to become a mommy saint myself. I love you, Paul.

About the Author

Kelly Ann Guest has been blessed with many opportunities to share God's love. She was a Dominican Sister of Saint Cecilia in Nashville, Tennessee, for five years, teaching at Saint Rose Academy in Birmingham, Alabama, and Saint Henry's in Nashville. Back home in Maryland, she taught middle school social studies, served as the education coordinator for a Catholic Charities program for pregnant teens, and as the Director of Religious Education at Our Lady of Fatima Church in Baltimore City. She is now a youth minister for her parish, Saint Bartholomew Church. Her greatest opportunity (and challenge), though, is being the mother of nine wonderful children and wife to one great guy. You can find her sipping lattes and writing at Nun2Nine.com and CatholicMom.com, on Facebook as Kelly Guest, and on Twitter and Instagram @nun2nine.